Conquering
THE HELL
CHAPTERS

Conquering THE HELL CHAPTERS

by
Annie Ruth

Unless otherwise indicated, all Scripture quotations are taken from the King James Version (KJV) of the Holy Bible. Public Domain.

Scripture quotations marked MSG are taken from THE MESSAGE, copyright © 1993, 2002, 2018 by Eugene H. Peterson. Used by permission of NavPress. All rights reserved. Represented by Tyndale House Publishers, Inc.

Copyright © 2021 by Annie Ruth
All rights reserved. No part of this book may be reproduced, scanned, or distributed in any printed or electronic form without permission.
First Edition: May 2021
Printed in the United States of America

ISBN: 978-0-9907390-2-9

To all of my sisters that have lifted me in prayer, loved me, encouraged me and supported me. I love you!

~ Annie Ruth

Table of Contents

Acknowledgement — ix
Preface — xi
Introduction — 1

PART ONE: THE HELL CHAPTERS
It's a Process – It's Hell Chapters — 15

Chapter 1	Get the hell out	19
Chapter 2	Who the hell are you?	25
Chapter 3	Put me through hell	29
Chapter 4	Going through hell	33
Chapter 5	Hot as hell	37
Chapter 6	What in (the) hell do you want	41
Chapter 7	Hell no	47
Chapter 8	A living hell	51
Chapter 9	Shut the hell up	53
Chapter 10	Catching hell	57
Chapter 11	Hell if I know	61
Chapter 12	Hell to pay	65
Chapter 13	Raising hell	69
Chapter 14	It hurts like hell	73
Chapter 15	Hellbent	77
Chapter 16	Knock the hell out of you	79

Chapter 17	All hell is breaking loose	83
Chapter 18	What the hell?	89
Chapter 19	Go to hell	93
Chapter 20	Like hell, I will	103
Chapter 21	Run like hell	107
Chapter 22	When hell freezes over	113
Chapter 23	Hellhole	119
Chapter 24	Been through hell	123
Chapter 25	Going to hell in a handbasket	127
Chapter 26	Crazy as hell	129
Chapter 27	To hell with it	131
Chapter 28	Come hell or high water	135
Chapter 29	Hellish	141
Chapter 30	Tired as hell	147

PART TWO: GOING DEEPER

Courage	153
Fear	156
Under Fire (Under Attack)	159
The Fire	163
Stop, Drop and Roll	167
<u>Activating the principles of stop, drop and roll</u>	
Stop	171
Drop	178
Roll	183
Closing prayer	191

Acknowledgement

To the Most High God— the *"I AM THAT I AM"*, who has empowered and inspired me to pour out from the depths of my soul.

Jude 24-25 (KJV)

[24] Now unto him that is able to keep you from falling, and to present you faultless before the presence of his glory with exceeding joy, [25] To the only wise God our Saviour, be glory and majesty, dominion, and power, both now and ever. Amen.

Thank you to all the sisters that have wrapped their arms around me in love— in prayer— in financial support— and in encouragement during some of the most turbulent times in my life.

To Dr. Kimya Moyo and **Dr. Karen Bankston** who were there to lift my arms physically and spiritually like Aaron and Hur lifted the hands of Moses during the battle.

"When Moses' hands grew tired, they took a stone and put it under him and he sat on it. Aaron and Hur held his hands up—one on one side, one on the other— so that his hands remained steady till sunset. So Joshua overcame the Amalekite army with the sword". (Exodus 17)

I also acknowledge the ministry of the late **Bishop Iona Locke.** [I did not know her personally.] When my brokenness had overcome me, I was reminded that *I was broken to minister—to help others—* and *I was broken to show that if God can heal me, he can heal you too!*

When my mother passed away in October 2020 it was listening to Bishop Iona Locke's exhortation on a song called *"Broken to Minister"* that was written by Damien Sneed, recorded on her Kingdom Victory LIVE (2012) project. This particular recording provided a spiritual release and healing for me that words cannot describe.

So, as strange as it may seem, I am thankful to this woman of God, posthumously, because her ministry and sermons was the catalyst that I needed to get back on my journey of releasing this book.

Finally, I honor the legacy of my mama, the late **Stella Hampton,** who taught me how to call on the name of *"Jesus"* as a young child. When I wasn't calling mama— I was always calling on Jesus. So, I sang to her—calling upon His name— as she departed this life.

"Jesus, Jesus, Jesus"

Preface

Sometimes we get so comfortable living our daily lives that we forget that we are in a spiritual war for our souls, with a lifetime of battles. As believers, we know that we will win the war but sometimes the battles are not always victorious.

Spiritual warfare is not always mystical and deep, and the devil does not appear with a fork and horns to attack us. Truth is— our everyday life is spiritual warfare, and we must see who the enemy really is.

Sometimes we may feel like other people are the enemy, but we must realize that the enemy is not flesh and blood. However, the enemy will use flesh and blood— even those who are closest to us, to attack us. His plan is to kill us and destroy the plan that God has for our lives.

John 10:10 (KJV)

[10] The thief cometh not, but for to steal, and to kill, and to destroy: I am come that they might have life, and that they might have it more abundantly.

The Bible tells us to *put on the whole armour of God.*

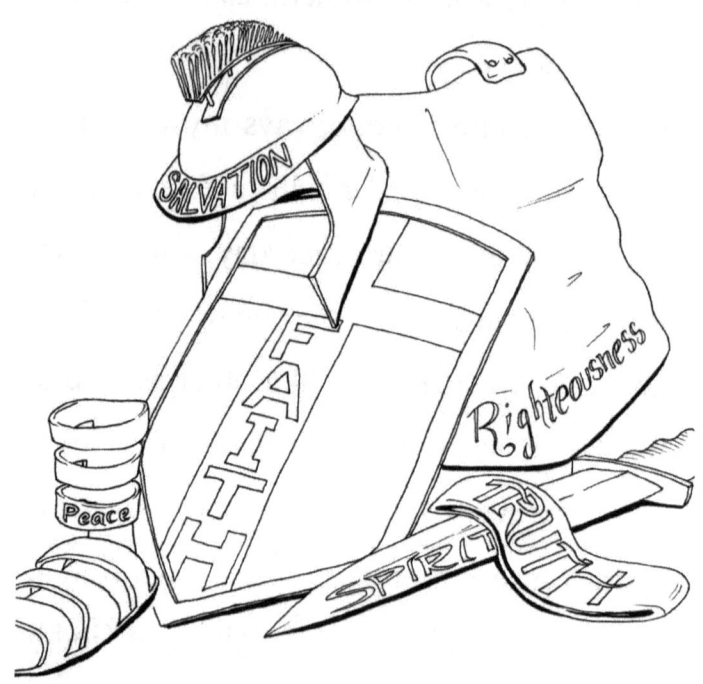

THE WHOLE ARMOUR OF GOD

Ephesians 6:10-18 (KJV)

¹⁰ Finally, my brethren, be strong in the Lord, and in the power of his might.

¹¹ Put on the whole armour of God, that ye may be able to stand against the wiles of the devil.

¹² For we wrestle not against flesh and blood, but against principalities, against powers, against the rulers of the darkness of this world, against spiritual wickedness in high places.

¹³ Wherefore take unto you the whole armour of God, that ye may be able to withstand in the evil day, and having done all, to stand.

¹⁴ Stand therefore, having your loins girt about with truth, and having on the breastplate of righteousness;

¹⁵ And your feet shod with the preparation of the gospel of peace;

¹⁶ Above all, taking the shield of faith, wherewith ye shall be able to quench all the fiery darts of the wicked.

¹⁷ And take the helmet of salvation, and the sword of the Spirit, which is the word of God:

¹⁸ Praying always with all prayer and supplication in the Spirit, and watching thereunto with all perseverance and supplication for all saints;

In **Ephesians 6:16** Quench means to extinguish—dousing or drowning out in water. The lesson that stands out for me the most is, we as believers must stand firm under the attack of the enemy and our faith is increased by hearing the Word of God.

Romans 10:17 (KJV)

¹⁷ So then faith cometh by hearing, and hearing by the word of God.

Introduction

"You don't smell like what you've been through", were the words that my sisterfriend said to me as we were driving down the street a few years ago. I knew exactly what she meant, and I warmly received her affirmation.

For the past few years, I have been experiencing some of the most trying times in my life. I refer to these trying times as my hell chapters. To be transparent, the end of my 35-year marriage and the work of rebuilding my life was at the forefront of my battles.

When I truly allowed the healing process to begin in my life, the hell chapters began to surface, and they kept coming. To be honest, it was overwhelming for me at first. I felt so many emotions. The first chapter that came to my mind several years ago was *"Get the Hell Out"*. That thought permeated my mind so much that I almost made it the title of this book. As I continued with my healing process, I realized that it was only one small chapter in my life and one small portion of my process. I also finally accepted the fact that I can help others more effectively if they know that I have been through some of the same stuff that they may be dealing with.

My prayer is that the chapters shared in this book will empower you and help you to conquer the hell chapters that you may be facing.

In my earlier writings, I shared my battle with low self-esteem, being mis-educated as a woman of African descent in America, being taunted about the darkness of my skin, and feeling unworthy of a father's love.

All these things left me with wounds and scars that did not heal until I was in my mid-thirties.

I chronicled my story in a poem that I wrote in 1982. That poem still resonates from my spirit today and I share it often with young people around the globe. The poem is:

A Black Woman, Nothing Else

There used to be a time when
I was ashamed of my skin.
I received tormenting jokes
From all of my friends.

*Of course, it wasn't done
To make me feel this way
But being black
Gave me much dismay.*

*"African, charcoal, Black Baby,"
I would hear.
But no one even noticed or knew
That I had silent tears.*

*Those names became nicknames and
I'd hear them every day at school
'cause when I was young and growing up
I'd play by my peers' rules.*

*One day when I was still young
My father left us all
And married a white woman
Who beckoned his every call.*

*I was really ashamed of my skin then,
I thought it was very bad,
I thought the white woman
Had something, which I could never have.*

*But one day when I was still young
I met a black lady darker than I was,
She cherished and boasted that her
Color was a gift from above.*

ANNIE RUTH

*She told me that I was beautiful -
Something no one had ever done.
She said, "Your skin is so black and smooth-
Which shows the perfecting of the sun."*

*She said, "To match the
Pretty black skin
Your teeth are white as snow
And I'm sure that you will show them
Everywhere that you go."*

*Every day she would tell me this
And her words began to spread.
They came from other people
I never even met.*

*The words of my friends changed to,
"Let me feel your face
And let me see you grin"-
For sister, you are beautiful-
Be proud of the color of your skin.*

*Now, I'm not ashamed of my skin
Though obstacles it may bring.
I proclaim to the world that I am
A Black Woman, the element of spring.*

*I blossom with happiness
And pride within myself
For I am A Black Woman*

And I wish to be nothing else.
---Annie Ruth

It was a poem of affirmation— words that reminded me that my feelings of not being worthy of a father's love or the feelings of shame and hurt were in my past. I had learned to leave them there— in the past.

That's why I began the poem with "There used to be a time," which signified that the worthless state of mind was a thought or condition of my past. I had left it behind— I had conquered it.

Well needless to say, when a marriage of thirty-five years ends, those feelings of doubt, shame and defeat came hurdling right back at me. I wrestled with feeling bad about myself— I questioned my womanhood and I had to learn how to re-affirm myself once more.

But something else occurred— I had to give myself permission and time to grieve and to heal. So today, I do not consider my divorce as the loss or death of a marriage, but I consider it as a new beginning.

Through my grieving and healing process, many

other hell chapters surfaced. As I continued to face those hell chapters, I was reminded that I would often have to encourage myself— I reminded myself not to hold back the rain because…

The rain purifies.

The rain nourishes.

The rain— (my tears)— were meant to cleanse me.

There was a time in my life when I could not cry. I wanted to release the pain and all the hurt, but no tears would come, or they came at a time when I felt that I could not allow myself to be vulnerable.

The tears came when I was in a crowded room amongst strangers. The tears came when I was talking about another subject. I tried to hold the tears in but one day the message came…

I heard the message loud and clear. It came to me as clear as I hear the birds chirping outdoors or the whistling of the wind… I heard the words, **"Let it Rain."**

Let it Rain
So what do I do when the tears are welling up in my

eyes— when I feel all of the hurt within my soul or even the joy of being thankful for the precious moments in time?
I let it rain.
I let the tears fall.
When the tears come, I let them fall.
At times I've tried to hold them back
When I needed to let them flow naturally—
"Let it rain," I say to my soul
The water cleanses and refreshes—
It makes whole again and
The water allows healing to take place.
It removes the dirt and debris—
Let it rain.
It's not a sign of weakness;
On the contrary, it reveals my strength.
The sun can't shine all of the time because
My garden will dry out without rain.
Let it rain.
I need to grow and heal and
My plants need to be revealed...
To a world— That can benefit from the fruit of
My labor.
Let it rain!
                        --Annie Ruth

Tears didn't just come for me. When I was going through the height of my pain and anger, I also thought about almost every *"Hell"* phrase that exists.

And although in its proper context hell is not considered a cuss word, it became one for me as the words and phrases raced through my mind. I never said them aloud but they raced through my mind— I heard them loudly. *"Hell"* in some of those thoughts could have even been used interchangeably with the "F- - -" bomb.

The first one that came was, *"Get the hell out!"*— You know that phrase when you are ready for someone to immediately get out of the building or room before you *knock the hell* out of him or her. Well, that is where I was. When the pain and hurtful feelings surfaced with each passing day, I asked the question, *"What in hell did you want?"* I felt as if I was *catching hell* and had *been through hell* all wrapped up together. I even realized that I was *hellbent* on trying to fight for a marriage all by myself and I had to make a decision to stop going down that that road; I deserved better— I deserved peace.

As I thought back about the lessons that many of the older women had shared about being the praying and loving wife, I thought about the many tests and trials... and the *"to death do us part"* and then came the thoughts of *"a living hell"*... And what to do *"when all hell is breaking loose"* in your home.

So, when I say the hell phrases came into my mind— they really came. Actually, they poured into my brain like a mighty stream. It was then that I realized that my experience wasn't just for me; I had to take every thought of hell and place it in its proper context — within a spiritual dimension.

GOING THROUGH ANOTHER PART OF HELL— THAT PLACE OF BROKENNESS

After going through all the hell that I went through for the past few years, I thought that I was clearly on my way to finally releasing my triumphant chapters. I felt that my journey was almost ready to share with the world but for some reason, I did not have a *"release"* in my spirit. The work on this book, literally came to a halt— a complete standstill. I could not understand why I did not have a desire to write but I knew that when it was time, I would pick the manuscript up and continue writing what God placed into my heart.

Then in 2020 during the height of a COVID-19 pandemic, my 89-year-old mother passed away—

There was nothing in the world that could have prepared me for the kind of pain that I felt, as I grieved her death. It wasn't the end of a 35-year marriage, but it was a hell that I never imagined. My mama has always been a part of my life and suddenly, at age fifty-seven, I had to adjust to the absence of her physical presence. Although I did not sorrow as one that did not have any hope, this loss was still devastating to me.

Her death was an awakening and I realized that I was still experiencing hell chapters but from a different perspective. *"Come hell or high water"* and *"it hurts like hell,"* took on a greater meaning for me. My mother's death felt as if I were in *"a press"*—a pressing of the oil of the Lord that had to be released in my life. So as the test and trials came to "press" me, *"I pressed"*.

Philippians 3:13-15 (KJV)

[13] Brethren, I count not myself to have apprehended: but this one thing I do, forgetting those things which are behind, and reaching forth unto those things which are before,

[14] I press toward the mark for the prize of the high calling of God in Christ Jesus.

I Pressed

To push down, up—strongly against
I press in both directions
Pressing down negativity
Pressing forward in growth...

Today was a press for me
I pushed hard to get here
This place of refreshing, empowerment and encouragement
A place where I can release— share and pour into others
I can empty my cup and I can be filled in one place

Today I pressed—

ANNIE RUTH

I pressed to move forward—to move in any direction
To rise above the pain
Like a barrel with the weight of the world sittin'
On top of me.
I pressed to find the positive.
I somehow felt that I had lost.
I pressed closer to His bosom.
To hear Him clearly
But most of all to listen and understand.
Today I pressed.

--Annie Ruth

Part 1
The Hell Chapters

IT'S A PROCESS, IT'S HELL CHAPTERS

At the beginning of each chapter, I will share the carnal, slang or surface meaning of some of these hell phrases and then delve into how God showed me to use the spiritual application in my life to conquer the hell chapters.

This book is not meant to counsel folks about problems or trials that they may experience in their lives. This book is one sister saying, "God will show you how to individually conquer the hell chapters in your life if you let Him". These seasons in my life have been a stretching for me but I have learned how to dig deep within myself and press forward, despite what it may feel like. I dig deep and I don't move in my own strength, but I press forward in the strength of the Lord. The Word that I stand upon is putting on the whole armour of God.

I remind myself that these battles (these hell chapters) are bigger than me and they are not always just about me.

Ephesians 6:10-12 (KJV)

¹⁰ Finally, my brethren, be strong in the Lord, and in the power of his might.

¹¹ Put on the whole armour of God, that ye may be able to stand against the wiles of the devil.

¹² For we wrestle not against flesh and blood, but against principalities, against powers, against the rulers of the darkness of this world, against spiritual wickedness in high places.

The peace of God keeps my mind. Whenever I get overwhelmed or to a place in my life where it feels like the fire has overcome my spirit, I dig deep within myself and I remind myself to meditate on God's Word— study God's Word—sing God's Word and allow it to minister to my heart and mind.

Isaiah 26:3 (KJV)

³ Thou wilt keep him in perfect peace, whose mind is stayed on thee: because he trusteth in thee.

Always remember— it is the peace of God that keeps our hearts and minds. We cannot conquer the hell chapters without the peace of God.

Philippians 4:6-8 (KJV)

⁶ Be careful for nothing; but in every thing by prayer and supplication with thanksgiving let your requests be made known unto God.

⁷ And the peace of God, which passeth all understanding, shall keep your hearts and minds through Christ Jesus.

⁸ Finally, brethren, whatsoever things are true, whatsoever things are honest, whatsoever things are just, whatsoever things are pure, whatsoever things are lovely, whatsoever things are of good report; if there be any virtue, and if there be any praise, think on these things.

I encourage you to dig deep within the Word of God and realize that you are not fighting your battles alone either. Remind yourself that you are fighting through the strength and might of Almighty God. You can conquer the hell chapters in your life. You are more than a conqueror.

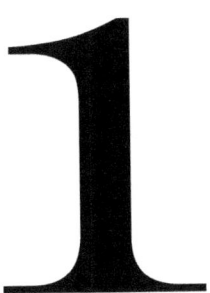

Get the hell out!

"Get the hell out" is an order for someone to leave quickly or suddenly. When a person has gotten to the point when they say, *"Get the hell out!"* that means that they have had more than enough— they cannot or will not take any more of how they are being treated or talked to.

One sister says, *"Get the hell out"* means get the hell out before I beat the hell out of you— take your stuff with you— Don't come back and don't make any plans to return. Typically, by the time someone tells a person this, the offender has had a chance to get it right. If a person is told "get the hell out" then that is the only option. The person telling you to get the hell out does not care if you have anywhere to go, you just have to get out. Get the hell out also means to escape quickly. If there is a fire in a building of place, someone will yell, "Get the hell out" as a command to do it immediately. On a lighter side, if someone gives you news about something that is unbelievable, *"get the hell out of here"* is also a way of saying, "NO WAY!"

In the Spirit "Get the Hell out!"

DEEP CLEANING MY HOUSE—

I went on a deep cleaning of my life and I began with that *sister in the mirror*. I began by ridding myself of toxins within my body, soul and spirit. I prayed the Word of God and took a real good look at myself.

Psalm 51:9-12 (KJV)

⁹Hide thy face from my sins, and blot out all mine iniquities.

¹⁰ Create in me a clean heart, O God; and renew a right spirit within me.

¹¹ Cast me not away from thy presence; and take not thy holy spirit from me.

¹² Restore unto me the joy of thy salvation; and uphold me with thy free spirit.

Acting like we don't need introspection—looking over our own lives—means that we are fooling ourselves. There is always an area of our lives that we can deeply clean.

1 John 1:8-10 (KJV)

⁸ If we say that we have no sin, we deceive ourselves, and the truth is not in us.

⁹ If we confess our sins, he is faithful and just to forgive us our sins, and to cleanse us from all unrighteousness.

¹⁰ If we say that we have not sinned, we make him a liar, and his word is not in us.

I prayed to God to clean my heart so that I could be able to serve Him with the right attitude and the right spirit. I prayed to God to fix my heart so that I would be a vessel that He could use. This prayer was poured out with a confessional spirit and was inspired by His Word.

In summation, *"Get the Hell Out"* is all about "cleaning our heart."

One song that resonates a great message of starting with oneself to change things is called, "Man in the Mirror," by the late Michael Jackson; (Songwriters: Glen Ballard and Siedah Garrett.)

The message of that song encouraged me to start with myself. In addition, a scripture that really brings this message home is:

Matthew 7:1-5 (KJV)
7 Judge not, that ye be not judged.

² For with what judgment ye judge, ye shall be judged: and with what measure ye mete, it shall be measured to you again.

³ And why beholdest thou the mote that is in thy brother's eye, but considerest not the beam that is in thine own eye?

⁴ Or how wilt thou say to thy brother, Let me pull out the mote out of thine eye; and, behold, a beam is in thine own eye?

⁵ Thou hypocrite, first cast out the beam out of thine own eye; and then shalt thou see clearly to cast out the mote out of thy brother's eye.

Although I experienced a situation in my life in which I was justified in telling someone to *"get the hell out,"* I didn't leave it there. I had taken a good hard look at myself as well. I looked at that sister in the mirror and that's how I was able to pray to God with a specific request— "Give ME a clean heart."

As we look at getting the "hell" out of our lives, another scripture really brings it home for me.

Galatians 5:9 (KJV)

⁹ A little leaven leaveneth the whole lump.

leav·en
noun

1) a substance, typically yeast, that is used in dough to make it rise.

2) cause (dough or bread) to rise by adding yeast or another leavening agent.

"It only takes a little bit of yeast to leaven the bread."

Sin, like leaven, grows and affects everything. So, we must get the hell out, and in other words—get the sin out because even allowing a little bit in will affect your entire being.

Who the hell are you?

This phrase is used when someone is clearly a stranger, or their behavior has altered so much that you don't recognize him or her. In normal circumstances, where strangers are not in your personal space, you wouldn't use this phrase but when someone who doesn't belong in your personal space has invaded it— you ask the question, *"Who the hell are you?"*

When someone that you know begins to do things out of his or her character and it is becoming a consistent problem then one would ask, *Who the hell are you?* When you ask someone *"who the hell are you?"* it means that the person has you all messed up— the person is acting in a way that is not their normal behavior. Sometimes the person may even be speaking to you in a demeaning and condescending way. *"Who the hell are you?"* is like saying, "have you lost your damn mind?"

In the Spirit "Who the hell are you?"

DEEP CLEANING MY HOUSE—

There have been times in my life when I have had to look inwardly and ask, *"Who are you?"* Those times when my character is not lining up with the individual that God created me to be. The Word of God reminds me that I am a new creation through Christ Jesus.

2 Corinthians 5:17 (KJV)

[17] Therefore if any man be in Christ, he is a new creature: old things are passed away; behold, all things are become new.

In my deep cleaning and reminding myself who I am, I must remember that I there must be a constant cleaning—a renewing of my mind.

Romans 12:1-2 (KJV)

12 I beseech you therefore, brethren, by the mercies of God, that ye present your bodies a living sacrifice, holy, acceptable unto God, which is your reasonable service.

² And be not conformed to this world: but be ye transformed by the renewing of your mind, that ye may prove what is that good, and acceptable, and perfect, will of God.

In my house cleaning, I am also reminded that my body is a temple of God's Spirit. Evil thoughts may come to my mind, but they can't stay there—I don't have to act upon them—and I definitely do not have to become someone who is not reflective of the Holy Spirit, that lives within me.

1 Corinthians 6:19-20 (KJV)

[19] What? know ye not that your body is the temple of the Holy Ghost, which is in you, which ye have of God, and ye are not your own?

[20] For ye are bought with a price: therefore, glorify God in your body, and in your spirit, which are God's.

3

Put me through hell

    This happens often in close relationships and we hear this phrase many times— from parents with children that have taken the wrong path in life. We have heard these words from spouses or significant others who have been treated wrong by the other person. We hear this phrase from loved ones who have to deal with a person with an addiction. You *put me through hell* is a way of describing a time when there is no peace in a person's life.

    The 'stuff' that a person endures takes him or her out of their comfort zone— into a place that, or experiences that, are unreal. Put through hell means you are tired, exhausted, and worn down. The other person's behavior is affecting you in a bad way.

In the Spirit "Put me through hell"

DEEP CLEANING MY HOUSE—

Put me through hell in the Spirit means that the test and trials have come to make me stronger— to bring me closer to God.

James 1:2-4 (KJV)

[2] My brethren, count it all joy when ye fall into divers temptations;

[3] Knowing this, that the trying of your faith worketh patience.

[4] But let patience have her perfect work, that ye may be perfect and entire, wanting nothing.

If there is an experience in our lives where we feel that someone put us through hell, we have the assurance in knowing that our Savior was tempted at all points (In all areas of life, yet without sin).

Hebrews 4:14-16 (KJV)

¹⁴ Seeing then that we have a great high priest, that is passed into the heavens, Jesus the Son of God, let us hold fast our profession.

¹⁵ For we have not an high priest which cannot be touched with the feeling of our infirmities; but was in all points tempted like as we are, yet without sin.

¹⁶ Let us therefore come boldly unto the throne of grace, that we may obtain mercy, and find grace to help in time of need.

Hebrews 4:14-16 (MSG)

¹⁴⁻¹⁶ Now that we know what we have—Jesus, this great High Priest with ready access to God—let's not let it slip through our fingers. We don't have a priest who is out of touch with our reality. He's been through weakness and testing, experienced it all—all but the sin. So, let's walk right up to him and get what he is so ready to give. Take the mercy, accept the help.

ANNIE RUTH

Going through hell

Going through hell means experiencing hard times. Going through means that you are enduring your test or most trying time. The everyday meaning of going through hell means you are experiencing pain. That pain can be mentally, physically or emotionally. Although going through hell is a process, it is hard to see the "this too shall pass" part of what you are going through. All you know is that it hurts.

In the Spirit "Going through hell"

DEEP CLEANING MY HOUSE—

APPLICATION: Reminders when you are going through hell. (1) This too shall pass. (2) It gets better (3) Fire burns off the impurities. There is a song that I love listening to called "Pure Gold," by The Clark Sisters (The song was written by Elbernita "Twinkie" Clark in the early 90's.)

The song compares our lives (our character) to silver or gold being put through the fire to bring out the impurities that exist. The words of the song remind us that the fire is not meant to destroy us but the fire is part of the process to help us establish a firm foundation in Christ Jesus.

Everything that we experience in life and every test and trial that we face is designed to teach us about ourselves. The learning process is like being polished. When we go through the fire successfully and we permit the process to allow us to identify the flaws in our character— we come out as PURE GOLD.

Example:

God is like the Refiner –

(noun). a person, device, or substance that removes

impurities, sediment, or other unwanted matter from something.

I am the Gold (The symbolic meaning of Gold) –

The color **gold** represents wealth, riches, and excess, and shares several of the same attributes of the color yellow. The color **gold** is developed by mixing the color yellow and the color brown, which is associated with illumination, love, compassion, courage, passion, and wisdom.

Gold (me) being put in the Refiner's fire is not meant to destroy the gold; the fire is designed to burn off the impurities.

Malachi 3:1-3 (KJV)

3 Behold, I will send my messenger, and he shall prepare the way before me: and the LORD, whom ye seek, shall suddenly come to his temple, even the messenger of the covenant, whom ye delight in: behold, he shall come, saith the LORD of hosts.

2 But who may abide the day of his coming? and who shall stand when he appeareth? for he is like a refiner's fire, and like fullers' soap:

3 And he shall sit as a refiner and purifier of silver: and he shall purify the sons of Levi, and purge them as gold and silver, that they may offer unto the Lord an offering in righteousness.

5

Hot as Hell

Hot as hell means the temperature is so hot in a place that you sweat profusely— It feels like there is no amount of water that can quench your thirst. In this place, the temperature is so hot that the only place that you can think of to compare the heat to is the center of a volcano or that place called *"hell"*.

In that place or situation in your life called *"Hot as hell"*, the temperature is uncomfortable, extreme and unpleasant. (As hell) intensifies the expression.

In the Spirit "Hot as hell"

DEEP CLEANING MY HOUSE—

Hot (fire) represents passion and service for Christ. Cold (ice) is the opposite of the spectrum. However, In Christ there is no middle ground. God doesn't want us to be a lukewarm church.

The problem with the church at Laodicea is the neutrality or lack of zeal (they are "lukewarm"). But their lukewarm state is not just about their passion about God. However, the lukewarm church (believer) has lost his or her dependence on God. In arrogance, he or she believes there is no need of Christ's righteousness because their doing it on their own.

Whenever we take pride in our own righteousness and our own doing, we are like lukewarm water and our self-righteousness is repulsive in the mouth of God.

Revelation 3:14-22 (MSG)

To Laodicea

¹⁴ Write to Laodicea, to the Angel of the church. God's Yes, the Faithful and Accurate Witness, the First of God's creation, says:

¹⁵⁻¹⁷ "I know you inside and out and find little to my liking. You're not cold, you're not hot—far better to be either cold or hot! You're stale. You're stagnant. You make me want to vomit. You brag, 'I'm rich, I've got it made, I need nothing from anyone,' oblivious that in fact you're a pitiful, blind beggar, threadbare and homeless.

¹⁸ "Here's what I want you to do: Buy your gold from me, gold that's been through the refiner's fire. Then you'll be rich. Buy your clothes from me, clothes designed in Heaven. You've gone around half-naked long enough. And buy medicine for your eyes from me so you can see, *really* see.

[19] "The people I love, I call to account—prod and correct and guide so that they'll live at their best. Up on your feet, then! About face! Run after God!

[20-21] "Look at me. I stand at the door. I knock. If you hear me call and open the door, I'll come right in and sit down to supper with you. Conquerors will sit alongside me at the head table, just as I, having conquered, took the place of honor at the side of my Father. That's my gift to the conquerors!

[22] "Are your ears awake? Listen. Listen to the Wind Words, the Spirit blowing through the churches."

6

What in (the) hell do you want?

What the hell? is defined as something that you ask when you are not happy with something and you want to know what is going on and why that situation is occurring. Typically, the phrase What the hell did (do) you want? Comes at a time of frustration and at a person's wits end. This phrase often is stated in relationships that have gone bad.

What in the hell This phrase is one of desperation and the cry of someone who is at his or her wits end. It is usually expressed when you have done all that you know to do, and circumstances still don't change. This phrase is also uttered when you don't want to be bothered with another person. That may be expressed by saying, "What the hell do you want"—emphasizing that you don't have the strength, ability or resources to give that person anything.

In the Spirit "What in (the) hell do you want"

DEEP CLEANING MY HOUSE—

There is nothing in hell that we, as believers, should want. Therefore, we should not live our lives like we are on a fast track to hell. If I believe that there is an eternal place of paradise after my life here on earth, then certainly there is a place of damnation.

Here are a few things about hell that stand out for me.

- Hell is hot.
- Hell is eternal.
- Hell is a place of misery and pain.

LUKE 16:19-24 (KJV)

[19] There was a certain rich man, which was clothed in purple and fine linen, and fared sumptuously every day:

[20] And there was a certain beggar named Lazarus, which was laid at his gate, full of sores,

[21] And desiring to be fed with the crumbs which fell from the rich man's table: moreover the dogs came and licked his sores.

[22] And it came to pass, that the beggar died, and was carried by the angels into Abraham's bosom: the rich man also died, and was buried;

[23] And in hell he lift up his eyes, being in torments, and seeth Abraham afar off, and Lazarus in his bosom.

[24] And he cried and said, Father Abraham, have mercy on me, and send Lazarus, that he may dip the tip of his finger in water, and cool my tongue; for I am tormented in this flame.

In summary, I don't want any parts of hell. I realize that I am responsible for my actions— the thoughts and the intents of my heart.

Matthew 5: 21 – 22 (KJV)

[21] Ye have heard that it was said of them of old time, Thou shalt not kill; and whosoever shall kill shall be in danger of the judgment:

[22] But I say unto you, That whosoever is angry with his brother without a cause shall be in danger of the judgment: and whosoever shall say to his brother, Raca, shall be in danger of the council: but whosoever shall say, Thou fool, shall be in danger of hell fire.

It is important that we are watchful and prayerful even in our Christian walk. We don't any part of hell. As we live our lives in a way that is pleasing to our Heavenly Father, we must always be aware that we are in a battle and the enemy will come in sheep's clothing to deceive us.

2 Peter 2:3-5 (MSG)

¹⁻² But there were also *lying* prophets among the people then, just as there will be lying religious teachers among you. They'll smuggle in destructive divisions, pitting you against each other—biting the hand of the One who gave them a chance to have their lives back! They've put themselves on a fast downhill slide to destruction, but not before they recruit a crowd of mixed-up followers who can't tell right from wrong.

²⁻³ They give the way of truth a bad name. They're only out for themselves. They'll say anything, *anything*, that sounds good to exploit you. They won't, of course, get by with it. They'll come to a bad end, for God has never just stood by and let that kind of thing go on.

⁴⁻⁵ God didn't let the rebel angels off the hook, but jailed them in hell till Judgment Day. Neither did he let the ancient ungodly world off. He wiped it out with a flood, rescuing only eight people—Noah, the sole voice of righteousness, was one of them.

ANNIE RUTH

Hell No!

This is one of those phrases that is expressed when the person wants to share his or her feeling of denial with the most passion. Simply saying "No" is not enough to get the point across, so "Hell no" is expressed to say emphatically No!

It is not just what you say but how you say it. In the movie, *The Color Purple*, when the mayor's wife asked Sofia (the character played by Oprah Winfrey) if she wanted to be her maid. Sofia responded with *"Hell No!"*— it was an insult to her to be asked to be someone's maid.

Hell no! is often used when people don't take a

simple "No" for the answer. The phrase means "Emphatically (forcefully) no!"—never! It is a command to stop asking me!

In the Spirit "Hell No!"

DEEP CLEANING MY HOUSE—

As I looked over my life and acknowledged the *unforgiveness* that was present in my heart, I had to ask myself the question—and be completely real with my own self—

Do you want to go to hell? (Hell No)—meaning I do not want that. I'm striving to be the daughter who my Heavenly Father is pleased with. I went to the Holy Scriptures to remind myself of what God wants for me.

Matthew 6:5- 15 (KJV)

⁵ And when thou prayest, thou shalt not be as the hypocrites are: for they love to pray standing in the synagogues and in the corners of the streets, that they may be seen of men. Verily I say unto you, They have their reward.

⁶ But thou, when thou prayest, enter into thy closet, and when thou hast shut thy door, pray to thy Father which is in secret; and thy Father which seeth in secret shall reward thee openly.

⁷ But when ye pray, use not vain repetitions, as the heathen do: for they think that they shall be heard for their much speaking.

⁸ Be not ye therefore like unto them: for your Father knoweth what things ye have need of, before ye ask him.

⁹ After this manner therefore pray ye: Our Father which art in heaven, Hallowed be thy name.

¹⁰ Thy kingdom come, Thy will be done in earth, as it is in heaven.

¹¹ Give us this day our daily bread.

¹² And forgive us our debts, as we forgive our debtors.

¹³ And lead us not into temptation, but deliver us from evil: For thine is the kingdom, and the power, and the glory, for ever. Amen.

14 For if ye forgive men their trespasses, your heavenly Father will also forgive you:

15 But if ye forgive not men their trespasses, neither will your Father forgive your trespasses.

8

A living hell

When everyday feels like the trials, tests and bad times will never end. When a person says this phrase, he or she feels like there is no sight of good times or good anything. Every day is negative and there is no hope of it ever ending.

In the Spirit "A living hell"

DEEP CLEANING MY HOUSE—
What I've realized is that the hell won't last forever. It will pass. The only way that the hell would last forever is if I were putting out "hell" into the universe. What God has said to me is sow good seeds… and don't be

weary in doing good. Keep doing good and good will come back to me.

Galatians 6:8-10 (KJV)

⁸ For he that soweth to his flesh shall of the flesh reap corruption; but he that soweth to the Spirit shall of the Spirit reap life everlasting.

⁹ And let us not be weary in well doing: for in due season we shall reap, if we faint not.

¹⁰ As we have therefore opportunity, let us do good unto all men, especially unto them who are of the household of faith.

Shut the hell up!

When a person gets to the point where they feel that all they are hearing is lies, stupidity, and total gibberish—the response is "Shut the hell up!"

This means don't say another word! Don't make a sound! I don't want to hear anything that you have to say. Sometimes we often say, "Shut the hell up" to the voices that we hear in our minds.

In the Spirit "Shut the hell up!"

DEEP CLEANING MY HOUSE—

From a Spiritual standpoint hell represents not only a

physical place but it represents the works of darkness.

There is a way that Jesus said "shut the hell up without cussing. [He said, "Get thee behind me Satan!"] This example came after his baptism by John the Baptist.

Luke 4: 1- 13 (KJV)

4 And Jesus being full of the Holy Ghost returned from Jordan, and was led by the Spirit into the wilderness,

² Being forty days tempted of the devil. And in those days he did eat nothing: and when they were ended, he afterward hungered.

³ And the devil said unto him, If thou be the Son of God, command this stone that it be made bread.

⁴ And Jesus answered him, saying, It is written, That man shall not live by bread alone, but by every word of God.

⁵ And the devil, taking him up into an high mountain, shewed unto him all the kingdoms of the world in a moment of time.

⁶ And the devil said unto him, All this power will I give thee, and the glory of them: for that is delivered unto me; and to whomsoever I will I give it.

⁷ If thou therefore wilt worship me, all shall be thine.

⁸ And Jesus answered and said unto him, Get thee behind me, Satan: for it is written, Thou shalt worship the Lord thy God, and him only shalt thou serve.

⁹ And he brought him to Jerusalem, and set him on a pinnacle of the temple, and said unto him, If thou be the Son of God, cast thyself down from hence:

¹⁰ For it is written, He shall give his angels charge over thee, to keep thee:

¹¹ And in their hands they shall bear thee up, lest at any time thou dash thy foot against a stone.

¹² And Jesus answering said unto him, It is said, Thou shalt not tempt the Lord thy God.

¹³ And when the devil had ended all the temptation, he departed from him for a season.

There are times (seasons) in our lives when we must tell the enemy to "get thee behind me Satan." It is basically telling him in the Spirit to (Shut the hell up)—get behind us!

10

Catching hell

Catching hell means experiencing bad times. Catching hell also means that one is being yelled at, retaliated against, or criticized in a demeaning way. Catching hell about something means that one has been reprimanded for doing or saying something to make someone else angry.

Catching hell is sometimes associated with "action and re-action" or "choice and consequences" A good example of this is the song *"I'm Catching Hell,"* by Natalie Cole (Songwriters: Chuck Jackson/Marvin Yancy). © Warner Chappell Music, Inc.

The writers of the song shares the story of a

woman who is no longer with her man and she is feeling regretful about the break-up. In the song, the woman says, "I'm catching hell" because she was experiencing some bad times without her man being there with her. She was lonely and had regrets because she had kicked him out. She had regrets that she ended a relationship over one intense argument. In the song, the woman used her words to say hurtful things to her man. She played the scene repeatedly in her mind and regretted that she told her man to leave. In the song she continuously expresses, "I'm catching hell".

"I'm catching hell" described what she was feeling and experiencing. She feeling lonely because of something that she describe as a bad decision that she had made regarding her relationship with her man.

In the Spirit "Catching hell"

DEEP CLEANING MY HOUSE—
Well, needless to say—in the Spirit the meaning of catching hell is far from Natalie Cole's reason. Catching

hell in the Spirit is suffering for Christ's sake.

1 Peter 3:13-18 (MSG)

¹³⁻¹⁸ If with heart and soul you're doing good, do you think you can be stopped? Even if you suffer for it, you're still better off. Don't give the opposition a second thought. Through thick and thin, keep your hearts at attention, in adoration before Christ, your Master. Be ready to speak up and tell anyone who asks why you're living the way you are, and always with the utmost courtesy. Keep a clear conscience before God so that when people throw mud at you, none of it will stick. They'll end up realizing that *they're* the ones who need a bath. It's better to suffer for doing good, if that's what God wants, than to be punished for doing bad. That's what Christ did definitively: suffered because of others' sins, the Righteous One for the unrighteous ones. He went through it all—was put to death and then made alive—to bring us to God.

Romans 8:18-19 (KJV)

¹⁸ For I reckon that the sufferings of this present time are not worthy to be compared with the glory which shall be revealed in us.

¹⁹ For the earnest expectation of the creature waiteth for the manifestation of the sons of God.

Suffering or experiencing bad times because I am a child of God comes with the territory of being His child. We don't catch hell because of "action and re-action" or "choice and consequence", we catch hell or we suffer because we are God's child and we have chosen to follow Him and His way. (In summation, the suffering is coming because of who I am.)

The scripture reminds us that catching hell is just a small part of the picture. The hard times that we experience in life because of who we are in Christ Jesus can't even be compared to the wonderful gifts God has prepared for us, as His children.

ROMANS 8:18-21 (MSG)

18-21 That's why I don't think there's any comparison between the present hard times and the coming good times. The created world itself can hardly wait for what's coming next. Everything in creation is being more or less held back. God reins it in until both creation and all the creatures are ready and can be released at the same moment into the glorious times ahead. Meanwhile, the joyful anticipation deepens.

11

Hell if I know

When you don't know the answer to what seems to be the easiest question. A genuine description that a person is lost. A dramatic way to say, "I don't know" or ask, "why am I going through this?" Hell if I know means something crazy or off the wall is going on.

In the Spirit "Hell if I know"

DEEP CLEANING MY HOUSE—

In the Spirit, "Hell if I know" focuses more on the simplest of things to confound the wise.

1 Corinthians 1:26 – 29 (KJV)

²⁶ For ye see your calling, brethren, how that not many wise men after the flesh, not many mighty, not many noble, are called:

²⁷ But God hath chosen the foolish things of the world to confound the wise; and God hath chosen the weak things of the world to confound the things which are mighty;

²⁸ And base things of the world, and things which are despised, hath God chosen, yea, and things which are not, to bring to nought things that are:

²⁹ That no flesh should glory in his presence.

Hell if I know in the Spirit is the perfect place for miracles to happen. One of the greatest miracles recorded in the scriptures is the feeding of the multitudes.

How did that happen? IT'S A MIRACLE.

Matthew 14:14 - 21 (KJV)

¹⁴ And Jesus went forth, and saw a great multitude, and was moved with compassion toward them, and he healed their sick.

¹⁵ And when it was evening, his disciples came to him, saying, This is a desert place, and the time is now past; send the multitude away, that they may go into the villages, and buy themselves victuals.

¹⁶ But Jesus said unto them, They need not depart; give ye them to eat.

¹⁷ And they say unto him, We have here but five loaves, and two fishes.

[18] He said, Bring them hither to me.

[19] And he commanded the multitude to sit down on the grass, and took the five loaves, and the two fishes, and looking up to heaven, he blessed, and brake, and gave the loaves to his disciples, and the disciples to the multitude.

[20] And they did all eat, and were filled: and they took up of the fragments that remained twelve baskets full.

[21] And they that had eaten were about five thousand men, beside women and children.

12

Hell to pay

If you say there'll be hell to pay, you are emphasizing that there will be serious trouble. Someone will be very angry if something happens.

In the Spirit "Hell to pay"

DEEP CLEANING MY HOUSE—
The wages of sin is death. In the Spirit, DEATH and HELL are the payment for those who have made sin their lifestyle – (A willing active practice.)

Galatians 6:8 (KJV)

⁸ For he that soweth to his flesh shall of the flesh reap corruption; but he that soweth to the Spirit shall of the Spirit reap life everlasting.

Oftentimes people talk about or ask the question, "How can a loving God send folks to hell?"

The answer is, God does not send us to hell—He gives us free will to choose or reject him. It's a choice.

DO I SERVE GOD OR DO I SERVE SIN?

Romans 6:23 (KJV)

²³ For the wages of sin is death; but the gift of God is eternal life through Jesus Christ our Lord.

God is loving and merciful but we cannot take advantage of His grace.

Ephesians 2:8 - 9 (KJV)

⁸ For by grace are ye saved through faith; and that not of yourselves: it is the gift of God:

⁹ Not of works, lest any man should boast.

Romans 6:1-2 (KJV)

6 What shall we say then? Shall we continue in sin, that grace may abound?

² God forbid. How shall we, that are dead to sin, live any longer therein?

Hell is the place that was created by God for the punishment of the devil and fallen angels (Matthew 25:41), and those whose names are not written in the book of life (Revelation 20:15).

BACKGROUND SCRIPTURE MATTHEW 25

Matthew 25:41 (KJV)

⁴¹ Then shall he say also unto them on the left hand, Depart from me, ye cursed, into everlasting fire, prepared for the devil and his angels:

BACKGROUND SCRIPTURE REVALATION 20

Revelation 20:15 (KJV)

¹⁵ And whosoever was not found written in the book of life was cast into the lake of fire.

ANNIE RUTH

13

Raising hell

To behave in a way that is not controlled and causes trouble. Raise hell can also mean to argue loudly or make demands. Emphasizing and protesting strongly in order to persuade people to correct or improve. Raising Hell means the person always has a negative response or rebuttal.

In the Spirit "Raising hell"

DEEP CLEANING MY HOUSE—
In the Spirit "Raising Hell" means purging and getting

the infection out of something. Sometimes when an object is seen getting larger, the viewer may attribute that increase in size to "growth" when in fact it can be something "swelling" like a boil with infection.

To eliminate a boil, the infection must be brought up out of it, usually using warm cloths and soaking in water. For us to be fit for God's use, we must be purged.

purge

1) rid (someone or something) of an unwanted quality, condition, or feeling.

2) remove in an abrupt or harsh way.

Psalm 51:6-8 (KJV)

[6] Behold, thou desirest truth in the inward parts: and in the hidden part thou shalt make me to know wisdom.

[7] Purge me with hyssop, and I shall be clean: wash me, and I shall be whiter than snow.

[8] Make me to hear joy and gladness; that the bones which thou hast broken may rejoice.

2 Timothy 2:19-26 (MSG)

¹⁹ Meanwhile, God's firm foundation is as firm as ever, these sentences engraved on the stones:

> GOD KNOWS WHO BELONGS TO HIM.
> STEER CLEAR OF EVIL, ALL YOU WHO NAME GOD AS GOD.

²⁰⁻²¹ In a well-furnished kitchen there are not only crystal goblets and silver platters, but waste cans and compost buckets—some containers used to serve fine meals, others to take out the garbage. Become the kind of container God can use to present any and every kind of gift to his guests for their blessing.

²²⁻²⁶ Run away from childish indulgence. Run after mature righteousness—faith, love, peace—joining those who are in honest and serious prayer before God. Refuse to get involved in inane discussions; they always end up in fights. God's servant must not be argumentative, but a gentle listener and a teacher who keeps cool, working firmly but patiently with those who refuse to obey. You never know how or when God might sober them up with a change of heart and a turning to the truth, enabling them to escape the Devil's trap, where they are caught and held captive, forced to run his errands.

14

It hurts like hell

The pain that you are experiencing is so bad that you can't find the words to describe it. If someone asked you to rate your pain like they do when you're in the hospital, you'd say that the pain is greater than that 1 – 10 scale that they give you. "It hurts like hell" is the best description of imagining your body on fire. This phrase describes all kinds of pain. Emotional pain, physical pain, and the torment of our souls.

In the Spirit "It hurts like hell"

DEEP CLEANING MY HOUSE—

Pain and suffering are as much a part of our lives as happiness and joy. However, when we are suffering because of nothing that we have done wrong, it is sometimes hard to accept it and we wonder "why me?"
I have found solace in knowing that God would not allow me to experience more pain than I am able to bear.

1 Corinthians 10:12-13 (KJV)

[12] Wherefore let him that thinketh he standeth take heed lest he fall.

[13] There hath no temptation taken you but such as is common to man: but God is faithful, who will not suffer you to be tempted above that ye are able; but will with the temptation also make a way to escape, that ye may be able to bear it.

Knowing that God believes in me helps me to press through the pain in my life. As a young woman, I would often listen to the song **"He Believes in Me"** by Dr. Bobby Jones & New Life (1982) The chorus of the song reminded me that like a natural parent, God believes in me. Knowing that God had my back gave me courage to move forward. I would often sing this song to myself and encourage myself with the Word of God. It helped me to press forward through the pain and trials in my life.

In the midst of whatever I am going through I realize that God believes in me and that He always has my back.

Psalm 34:6-7 (KJV)

⁶ This poor man cried, and the LORD heard him, and saved him out of all his troubles.

⁷ The angel of the LORD encampeth round about them that fear him, and delivereth them.

I also accept the fact that I am not perfect and that many things happen in my life because that test is to help make me— and shape who I am to become.

Romans 8:18 (KJV)

¹⁸ For I reckon that the sufferings of this present time are not worthy to be compared with the glory which shall be revealed in us.

ANNIE RUTH

15

Hellbent

Hellbent means that you are doing what you set out to do no matter what happens. It is an attitude of determination that you have personalized— much like hell or high water.

In the Spirit "Hellbent"

DEEP CLEANING MY HOUSE—

In the Spirit, Hellbent represents the kind of determination that we must have to live victorious in Christ Jesus. That's the kind of attitude that we must have as we live our lives.

Romans 8:38-39 (KJV)

³⁸ For I am persuaded, that neither death, nor life, nor angels, nor principalities, nor powers, nor things present, nor things to come,

³⁹ Nor height, nor depth, nor any other creature, shall be able to separate us from the love of God, which is in Christ Jesus our Lord.

16

Knock the hell out of you

This phrase is interchangeable with "I'm going to hit you so hard that you're going to straighten up. Knocking the hell out of someone means that when that person comes to consciousness, he or she will be "right".

In the Spirit "Knock the hell out of you"

DEEP CLEANING MY HOUSE—

"I'm gonna knock the hell out of you" is the kind of mentality that we should have when we are fighting

the enemy— when we are fighting against the darkness of this world. (The devil and his imps). However, we must keep in mind that in spiritual warfare— We are not fighting individuals in the natural, so our weapons won't be natural weapons— Our weapons are spiritual weapons.

2 Corinthians 10:3-5 (KJV)

³ For though we walk in the flesh, we do not war after the flesh:

⁴ (For the weapons of our warfare are not carnal, but mighty through God to the pulling down of strong holds;)

⁵ Casting down imaginations, and every high thing that exalteth itself against the knowledge of God, and bringing into captivity every thought to the obedience of Christ;

So, what are our weapons? Our weapons are the whole armor of God.

- Belt of Truth

- Breastplate of righteousness
- Feet covered with the Gospel of Peace
- Shield of Faith
- The helmet of salvation

Ephesians 6:10 – 18 (KJV)

[10] Finally, my brethren, be strong in the Lord, and in the power of his might.

[11] Put on the whole armour of God, that ye may be able to stand against the wiles of the devil.

[12] For we wrestle not against flesh and blood, but against principalities, against powers, against the rulers of the darkness of this world, against spiritual wickedness in high places.

[13] Wherefore take unto you the whole armour of God, that ye may be able to withstand in the evil day, and having done all, to stand.

[14] Stand therefore, having your **loins girt about with truth,** and having on the **breastplate of righteousness;**

[15] And your **feet shod with the preparation of the gospel of peace;**

16 Above all, **taking the shield of faith**, wherewith ye shall be able to quench all the fiery darts of the wicked.

17 And take the **helmet of salvation**, and the sword of the Spirit, which is the word of God:

18 Praying always with all prayer and supplication in the Spirit, and **watching thereunto with all perseverance and supplication for all saints;**

The actions that we take in battle are:

- Praying with the leading of the Holy Spirit;

- And watching for all of the people of God.

Romans 8:26-27 (KJV)

26 Likewise the Spirit also helpeth our infirmities: for we know not what we should pray for as we ought: but the Spirit itself maketh intercession for us with groanings which cannot be uttered.

27 And he that searcheth the hearts knoweth what is the mind of the Spirit, because he maketh intercession for the saints according to the will of God.

17

All hell is breaking loose

This phrase means that there is total chaos. Everything around you is in disarray. The situations seem similar to a water main break or the releasing of a large dam. This term is used to describe what happens when violent, destructive, and confused activity suddenly begins.

In the Spirit "All hell is breaking loose"

DEEP CLEANING MY HOUSE—

There are times when we have to speak directly to the

storms in our lives or (all the hell breaking loose in our lives)... and say "LOOSE", like the saints of old. Jesus demonstrated this by example in his words "...Peace, be still".

Mark 4:37-39 (KJV)

[37] And there arose a great storm of wind, and the waves beat into the ship, so that it was now full.

[38] And he was in the hinder part of the ship, asleep on a pillow: and they awake him, and say unto him, Master, carest thou not that we perish?

[39] And he arose, and rebuked the wind, and said unto the sea, Peace, be still. And the wind ceased, and there was a great calm.

I can remember when I had to apply the peace of God when all hell was breaking loose in my life. In 1988 when I was giving birth to my first child, he wasn't getting enough oxygen in the womb and the doctor had to deliver my child through an emergency cesarean procedure. That was far from the delivery that I had planned. My goal was to have a nurse midwife deliver my child with a natural childbirth without any anesthesia. Well, it's obvious that the natural childbirth plan didn't happen. In that delivery room at that time— all hell was breaking loose.

I am a firm believer that the Word of God allows us to focus on the peace of God when all hell is breaking loose— no matter what that hell may be.

Isaiah 26:3 (KJV)

³ Thou wilt keep him in perfect peace, whose mind is stayed on thee: because he trusted in thee.

Everything happened so fast in that delivery room. All I had time to say before they administered the anesthesia was "Lord, Cameron and I are in your hands."— I truly had the peace of God in that experience.

Philippians 4:6-8 (KJV)

⁶ Be careful for nothing; but in every thing by prayer and supplication with thanksgiving let your requests be made known unto God.

⁷ And the peace of God, which passeth all understanding, shall keep your hearts and minds through Christ Jesus.

⁸ Finally, brethren, whatsoever things are true, whatsoever things are honest, whatsoever things are just, whatsoever things are pure, whatsoever things are lovely, whatsoever things are of good report; if there be any virtue, and if there be any praise, think on these things.

When I awoke from the anesthesia, I was informed that my newborn baby had experienced a stroke and he had ingested the meconium (a baby's first bowel movement) into his lungs. My newborn had tubes going into various parts of his body, but I had the peace of God. The doctors said, *"...parts of his brain had died because of the stroke,"* but I had the peace of God. The doctors said, *"...your baby won't be able to nurse or drink from a bottle,"* but I had the peace of God. Through every bad report that the doctor brought to me, I had the perfect peace of God. That **perfect peace** didn't mean that I didn't understand my situation. That perfect peace meant that through it all— through all of the hell breaking loose in my life— I chose to rest in the peace of God.

I actively applied **_Philippians 4:6 – 8_** that I listed above. I prayed and trusted that God would handle His end and I would handle my end.

When all hell was breaking loose, I chose to focus on the good—and the promises of God. For that particular "hell breaking loose" phase of my life, I stood upon His Word that says,

Isaiah 53:4-5 (KJV)

[4] Surely he hath borne our griefs, and carried our sorrows: yet we did esteem him stricken, smitten of God, and afflicted.

[5] But he was wounded for our transgressions, he was bruised for our iniquities: the chastisement of our peace was upon him; and with his stripes we are healed.

I actively applied His Word. I had thought and even audibly spoken the prayer for my child and myself. I had blessed my child and even anointed him with oil. And although I realized that all hell was breaking loose, I also knew that whatever I magnified, that is what I would focus on. So, I chose to focus on the peace of God and be intentional about thinking on the good things.

Mark 16:17-18 (KJV)

¹⁷ And these signs shall follow them that believe; In my name shall they cast out devils; they shall speak with new tongues;

¹⁸ They shall take up serpents; and if they drink any deadly thing, it shall not hurt them; they shall lay hands on the sick, and they shall recover.

18

What the hell?

A person asks this question when he or she is in shock or amazement. When a situation catches someone off guard and that individual has no words to describe his or her disbelief or astonishment, in some cases.

This is a question that is asked when a person is not happy with something and he or she wants to know what is going on and why that situation is occurring.

What the hell is an intense form of WHAT? This is also a reaction to something strange or abnormal.

In the Spirit "What the hell"

DEEP CLEANING MY HOUSE—

Sometimes *What the hell?* is an indication of shock and disgust of seeing those professing to be of God not truly being His.

There is blatant disobedience prevalent in our world today. Much of this disobedience and perversion is occurring within the organization of the church. The Bible speaks very clearly about what will happen when this occurs.

Matthew 7:15-23 (KJV)

[15] Beware of false prophets, which come to you in sheep's clothing, but inwardly they are ravening wolves.

[16] Ye shall know them by their fruits. Do men gather grapes of thorns, or figs of thistles?

[17] Even so every good tree bringeth forth good fruit; but a corrupt tree bringeth forth evil fruit.

18 A good tree cannot bring forth evil fruit, neither can a corrupt tree bring forth good fruit.

19 Every tree that bringeth not forth good fruit is hewn down and cast into the fire.

20 Wherefore by their fruits ye shall know them.

21 Not every one that saith unto me, Lord, Lord, shall enter into the kingdom of heaven; but he that doeth the will of my Father which is in heaven.

22 Many will say to me in that day, Lord, Lord, have we not prophesied in thy name? and in thy name have cast out devils? and in thy name done many wonderful works?

23 And then will I profess unto them, I never knew you: depart from me, ye that work iniquity.

ANNIE RUTH

19

Go to hell

"Go to Hell" used to show that one is extremely angry with someone. Sometimes people use this phrase as a command to shut-up— ordering an individual not to say another word. (2) The phrase is used when something becomes completely ruined or (3) When an effort has failed completely.

Go to hell is an expression of anger or contempt. It means "get out of here!—Go away and leave me alone. Go to hell is an angry response to a question asked.

In the Spirit "Go to hell"

DEEP CLEANING MY HOUSE—

Hell = Home to the devil (When using it in this way, it would not be considered a cuss word.)

Jesus gives us a clear demonstration on where to tell Satan (the devil) to go.

> **Luke 4:8**
> **And Jesus answered and said unto him, Get thee behind me, Satan: for it is written, Thou shalt worship the Lord thy God, and him only shalt thou serve.**

Luke 4: 1-14 (KJV)

4 And Jesus being full of the Holy Ghost returned from Jordan, and was led by the Spirit into the wilderness,

² Being forty days tempted of the devil. And in those days he did eat nothing: and when they were ended, he afterward hungered.

³ And the devil said unto him, If thou be the Son of God, command this stone that it be made bread.

⁴ And Jesus answered him, saying, It is written, That man shall not live by bread alone, but by every word of God.

⁵ And the devil, taking him up into an high mountain, shewed unto him all the kingdoms of the world in a moment of time.

⁶ And the devil said unto him, All this power will I give thee, and the glory of them: for that is delivered unto me; and to whomsoever I will I give it.

⁷ If thou therefore wilt worship me, all shall be thine.

⁸ And Jesus answered and said unto him, Get thee behind me, Satan: for it is written, Thou shalt worship the Lord thy God, and him only shalt thou serve.

⁹ And he brought him to Jerusalem, and set him on a pinnacle of the temple, and said unto him, If thou be the Son of God, cast thyself down from hence:

¹⁰ For it is written, He shall give his angels charge over thee, to keep thee:

¹¹ And in their hands they shall bear thee up, lest at any time thou dash thy foot against a stone.

¹² And Jesus answering said unto him, It is said, Thou shalt not tempt the Lord thy God.

¹³ And when the devil had ended all the temptation, he departed from him for a season.

¹⁴ And Jesus returned in the power of the Spirit into Galilee: and there went out a fame of him through all the region round about.

We are shown what our response should be when the enemy comes in to tempt us. We've got to fight the enemy with the Word of God. (With a clear understanding and clarity of how we are using the Word of God!) As believers, we have both the authority and the power to cast the devil out. Jesus shared with His disciples and we have that Word to stand upon, even today, that greater work shall we do.

Mark 16:17-20 (KJV)

¹⁷ And these signs shall follow them that believe; In my name shall they cast out devils; they shall speak with new tongues;

¹⁸ They shall take up serpents; and if they drink any deadly thing, it shall not hurt them; they shall lay hands on the sick, and they shall recover.

¹⁹ So then after the Lord had spoken unto them, he was received up into heaven, and sat on the right hand of God.

²⁰ And they went forth, and preached every where, the Lord working with them, and confirming the word with signs following. Amen.

It is important that we realize that the Word of God is our weapon, but we also need to know how to understand and use our weapon too!

Notice in these particular verses above, Satan attempted to mis-represent the scriptures against Jesus in this temptation account. So, it's not just enough to quote the scriptures, we have to live and have a clear understanding of how to apply the Word of God in our lives and within the battles that we face.

James 4:7 (KJV)

⁷ Submit yourselves therefore to God. Resist the devil, and he will flee from you.

So as much as we have the power and authority to cast the devil out, we don't always have to audibly tell the devil to go somewhere. There is power in our resisting.

The Message Bible interpretation of this scripture really breaks it down.

James 4:4-10 (MSG)
Get Serious

⁴⁻⁶ You're cheating on God. If all you want is your own way, flirting with the world every chance you get, you end up enemies of God and his way. And do you suppose God doesn't care? The proverb has it that "he's a fiercely jealous lover." And what he gives in love is far better than anything else you'll find. It's common knowledge that "God goes against the willful proud; God gives grace to the willing humble."

7-10 So let God work his will in you. Yell a loud *no* to the Devil and watch him make himself scarce. Say a quiet *yes* to God and he'll be there in no time. Quit dabbling in sin. Purify your inner life. Quit playing the field. Hit bottom and cry your eyes out. The fun and games are over. Get serious, really serious. Get down on your knees before the Master; it's the only way you'll get on your feet.

There are also times that we must fight the enemy with *"prayer and fasting"*. Sometimes the battles are more intense, and we must intensify our weapons.

Mark 9:29 (KJV)

[29] And he said unto them, This kind can come forth by nothing, but by prayer and fasting.

BACKGROUND SCRIPTURE
Mark 9:15-29 (KJV)

[15] And straightway all the people, when they beheld him, were greatly amazed, and running to him saluted him.

16 And he asked the scribes, What question ye with them?

17 And one of the multitude answered and said, Master, I have brought unto thee my son, which hath a dumb spirit;

18 And wheresoever he taketh him, he teareth him: and he foameth, and gnasheth with his teeth, and pineth away: and I spake to thy disciples that they should cast him out; and they could not.

19 He answereth him, and saith, O faithless generation, how long shall I be with you? how long shall I suffer you? bring him unto me.

20 And they brought him unto him: and when he saw him, straightway the spirit tare him; and he fell on the ground, and wallowed foaming.

21 And he asked his father, How long is it ago since this came unto him? And he said, Of a child.

22 And ofttimes it hath cast him into the fire, and into the waters, to destroy him: but if thou canst do any thing, have compassion on us, and help us.

23 Jesus said unto him, If thou canst believe, all things are possible to him that believeth.

24 And straightway the father of the child cried out, and said with tears, Lord, I believe; help thou mine unbelief.

25 When Jesus saw that the people came running together, he rebuked the foul spirit, saying unto him, Thou dumb and deaf spirit, I charge thee, come out of him, and enter no more into him.

26 And the spirit cried, and rent him sore, and came out of him: and he was as one dead; insomuch that many said, He is dead.

27 But Jesus took him by the hand, and lifted him up; and he arose.

28 And when he was come into the house, his disciples asked him privately, Why could not we cast him out?

29 And he said unto them, This kind can come forth by nothing, but by prayer and fasting.

ANNIE RUTH

20

Like hell, I will

"Like hell, I will", means *"You must be crazy if you think I'm gonna do that..."*

The phrase suggests that the speaker feels insulted by the request. This phrase emphasizes strong disagreement and strong opposition to something. It is another way of saying "Hell no!"

In the Spirit "Like hell, I will"

DEEP CLEANING MY HOUSE—

Strong disagreement and opposition also convey this phrase in the Spirit. There are principles that we must hold firm to in our lives. Although I've touched on this topic in the earlier **Hell No** chapter, I must address it again.

Unforgiveness always returns to the forefront when we are getting the hell out of our lives in the Spirit. The negative of not forgiving can lead to emotional turmoil, hate, resentment, and bitterness. Unforgiveness can even create health issues and stop us from experiencing the freedom that forgiveness brings.

On a personal note, I've been at that place where bitterness had rooted itself within me so much that I began to claim it as part of my personality. Believe me—that's something that you don't want in your life.

The other harsh reality is that we tie God's hands when unforgiveness is present in our lives.

Matthew 6:14-15 (MSG)

¹⁴⁻¹⁵ In prayer there is a connection between what God does and what you do. You can't get forgiveness from God, for instance, without also forgiving others. If you refuse to do your part, you cut yourself off from God's part.

Sometimes the bitterness has been in our hearts for so long that we don't recognize it. We will say that we are not bitter, but we are. The bitterness has been there for so long that it has become a part of our being. It truly takes God to reveal it to us.

Psalm 139:1-3 (KJV)

139 O lord, thou hast searched me, and known me.

² Thou knowest my downsitting and mine uprising, thou understandest my thought afar off.

³ Thou compassest my path and my lying down, and art acquainted with all my ways.

OUR PRAYER

Lord, search my heart. Help me to see you clearly—your will—your way and help me to align my heart with your heart. Help me to do what is pleasing in your sight. Help me to honor the Holy Spirit within me—this gift that you have given me to live and be a witness of YOU.

Ephesians 4:30-32 (KJV)

[30] And grieve not the holy Spirit of God, whereby ye are sealed unto the day of redemption.

[31] Let all bitterness, and wrath, and anger, and clamour, and evil speaking, be put away from you, with all malice:

[32] And be ye kind one to another, tenderhearted, forgiving one another, even as God for Christ's sake hath forgiven you.

21

Run like hell

Run as fast or as hard as you can, like in a race with a prize being the end goal. (2) Run as fast as you can to get away from something that you do not want to overtake you.

In the Spirit "Run like hell"

DEEP CLEANING MY HOUSE—

My walk with the Lord is like a race that I am running. When I was a child, we often sang an old congregational song titled, *"I'm running for my life"* (Public Domain). The original author is unknown but the song has lasted across generations because of the timeless message of running for Jesus. The song is a classic Negro Folk song from the early 1900's, which was passed down from generation to generation and sung throughout the early Black church.

The song originally appeared in a recorded version on a compilation called *Negro Religious Field Recordings from Louisiana, Mississippi, Tennessee* Vol. 1 1934-1942.
Rev. McGhee is credited for leading "I'm running for my life", a call and response song.

Because of the traumatic experience of slavery, *run like hell* is something that many folks of African descent can relate to.

The words of *"I'm running for my life,"* state,
"I'm running for my life
I'm running for my life (repeat 4x)
If anybody ask you,
what's the matter with me

Tell 'em I'm saved, sanctified

Holy Ghost filled and fire baptized

I've got Jesus on my side

And I'm running for my life."

Hebrews 12:1-2 (KJV)

12 Wherefore seeing we also are compassed about with so great a cloud of witnesses, let us lay aside every weight, and the sin which doth so easily beset us, and let us run with patience the race that is set before us,

² Looking unto Jesus the author and finisher of our faith; who for the joy that was set before him endured the cross, despising the shame, and is set down at the right hand of the throne of God.

Another way of looking at this phrase in the Spirit is *"Live your life— giving it your best— everyday"*—Living like each day was your last day!

Ecclesiastes 9:10-12 (KJV)

[10] Whatsoever thy hand findeth to do, do it with thy might; for there is no work, nor device, nor knowledge, nor wisdom, in the grave, whither thou goest.

[11] I returned, and saw under the sun, that the race is not to the swift, nor the battle to the strong, neither yet bread to the wise, nor yet riches to men of understanding, nor yet favour to men of skill; but time and chance happeneth to them all.

One of the scriptures in the bible that I can recall someone running or fleeing from something was in the Old Testament when Joseph ran from Potiphar's wife because she was making sexual advances towards him. He ran because he saw that that was the only way for him to get out of that situation immediately.

Genesis 39:10 - 12 (KJV)

[10] And it came to pass, as she spake to Joseph day by day, that he hearkened not unto her, to lie by her, or to be with her.

¹¹ And it came to pass about this time, that Joseph went into the house to do his business; and there was none of the men of the house there within.

¹² And she caught him by his garment, saying, Lie with me: and he left his garment in her hand, and fled, and got him out.

In the New Testament, the Word of God also tells us to flee fornication— reminding us that our bodies are temples of God's Spirit.

1 Corinthians 6:17-19 (KJV)

¹⁷ But he that is joined unto the Lord is one spirit.

¹⁸ Flee fornication. Every sin that a man doeth is without the body; but he that committeth fornication sinneth against his own body.

¹⁹ What? know ye not that your body is the temple of the Holy Ghost which is in you, which ye have of God, and ye are not your own?

In this time of reflecting on the hell chapters in my life, I am reminded that my body is a temple of the Holy Ghost.

My run is not always fleeing evilness; my run is my life and what is reflected in it. The saints of old use to sing this call and response song that the leader says, *"I believe I'll run on"*. The congregation responded with *"See what the end's gonna be"*. The saints would continue with that verse over and over again until the church sang themselves happy with shouting, dancing and rejoicing. The leader would add new call but the response would remain the same. *("See what the end's gonna be")*

"I believe I'll pray on"— "fast on"— "shout on" and so on, outlining elements to encourage one's self to keep running the race for Jesus. (Living for God.)

22

When hell freezes over

"When hell freezes over" is used to say that one thinks that something will <u>never</u> happen. Sometimes people use this phrase to describe something that he or she will vow *not to do*. This statement dates back from the early 1900s. It is a hyperbole— an exaggerated statement not meant to be taken literally. The statement suggests *"It will never happen"*.

In the Spirit "When hell freezes over"

DEEP CLEANING MY HOUSE—

When I thought about things that will never happen with God, I thought immediately of His faithfulness and the other characteristics of our Creator that resonate within me are:

God will never lie

God will never change—our Savior is authentic.

When hell freezes over in the Spirit says, God is faithful—He will never lie—and He doesn't change. So how does this apply to my life?

God's faithfulness is activated when I'm honest with where I am and what I have allowed into my life.

1 John 1:8-10 (KJV)

⁸ If we say that we have no sin, we deceive ourselves, and the truth is not in us.

⁹ If we confess our sins, he is faithful and just to forgive us our sins, and to cleanse us from all unrighteousness.

¹⁰ If we say that we have not sinned, we make him a liar, and his word is not in us.

Acknowledging where I truly am—and that there is sin and iniquity in my life is important. If I don't acknowledge that the sin is there and ask for His forgiveness, then I will never experience the faithfulness of his forgiveness.

One thing that I am sure of is that I am a child of the Most High God. Being His daughter requires me to live circumspect. I must always realize that I am in a war. Battles will always be present in my life and I must be vigilant to guard my heart.

Ephesians 5:14-16 (KJV)

¹⁴ Wherefore he saith, Awake thou that sleepest, and arise from the dead, and Christ shall give thee light.

¹⁵ See then that ye walk circumspectly, not as fools, but as wise,

¹⁶ Redeeming the time, because the days are evil.

So, if I said, "God will lie when Hell freezes over",

that would be an accurate description of His character— *for He cannot lie*— He will never lie!

Numbers 23:19 (KJV)

[19] God is not a man, that he should lie; neither the son of man, that he should repent: hath he said, and shall he not do it? or hath he spoken, and shall he not make it good?

One thing I've learned through experiencing my hell chapters is that Jesus—Our Saviour. God's only begotten son never changes. That which has been promised shall be performed.

God never changing means that His Love last forever. God is immutable— an attribute that "God is unchanging in his character, will, and covenant promises."

Many theologians use three major characteristics of God— omnipotence (all powerful), omniscience (all knowing), and omnipresence (always everywhere).

This is the assuredness that I can stand on, even in my darkest hour. Just like God was there for His children in the Old and New Testament, He is there for me.

Hebrews 13:8 (KJV)

⁸ Jesus Christ the same yesterday, and to day, and for ever.

Hebrews 13:8 (MSG)
⁸For Jesus doesn't change—yesterday, today, tomorrow, he's always totally himself.

# 23

Hellhole

A hellhole describes a place where nothing is right—there are bugs, rats—it's dirty and all kinds of deviant folks are in there. It is a place that you don't want to live.

Hellhole can also describe a place where a lot of hell is going on all the time— fighting and confusion all the time – Nothing positive and no peace.

In the Spirit "Hellhole"

DEEP CLEANING MY HOUSE—

There is nowhere that I can mentally or physically go that

God won't be there! In those places where I feel alone and forsaken—

He is there!

Those places in my life that feel like it is desolate—

He is there!

When I'm in the deepest pit—

He is there!

Psalm 139:7-9 (KJV)

[7] Whither shall I go from thy spirit? or whither shall I flee from thy presence?

[8] If I ascend up into heaven, thou art there: if I make my bed in hell, behold, thou art there.

[9] If I take the wings of the morning, and dwell in the uttermost parts of the sea;

"Hell Hole" is descriptive of an environment, surrounding or situation that we can find ourselves in and not always of our own choosing.

I can recall in Daniel 3 where God's chosen Hebrew boys Shadrach, Meshach, and Abednego (Hananiah, Mishael, and Azariah) were thrown in the blazing hot furnace because they didn't fall down to worship the King Nebuchadnezzar's gold idol. This scripture shows me that God will be there for us even amid our "hell holes".

BACKGROUND SCRIPTURE: Daniel 3

Daniel 3:21-25 (KJV)

²¹ Then these men were bound in their coats, their hosen, and their hats, and their other garments, and were cast into the midst of the burning fiery furnace.

²² Therefore because the king's commandment was urgent, and the furnace exceeding hot, the flames of the fire slew those men that took up Shadrach, Meshach, and Abednego.

²³ And these three men, Shadrach, Meshach, and Abednego, fell down bound into the midst of the burning fiery furnace.

²⁴ Then Nebuchadnezzar the king was astonished, and rose up in haste, and spake, and said unto his counsellors, Did not we cast three men bound into the midst of the fire? They answered and said unto the king, True, O king.

²⁵ He answered and said, Lo, I see four men loose, walking in the midst of the fire, and they have no hurt; and the form of the fourth is like the Son of God.

Been Through Hell

Someone has suffered a lot. It is in the past—you have come out of it.

In the Spirit "Been through hell"

DEEP CLEANING MY HOUSE—

Our trials come to make us stronger—we won't stay in the trial forever. Been through hell in the spirit means that I am an overcomer. Been through Hell means I can look back and clearly see where God has brought me from. Hell was something that I went through but it was not my destination.

Those old spiritual and religious songs that our ancestors sang in those back woods gatherings of believers still resonate today. One song that I would often hear my the saint of old sing is "Look where He brought me from—brought me out of darkness into the marvelous light—look where he brought me from.

I even sing this song today. This song affirms that "I've been through hell but God didn't leave me there. The song says that I have been through a test— but now I am singing my testimony. "Look where He brought me from."

1 Peter 5:10-11 (MSG)

[8-11] Keep a cool head. Stay alert. The Devil is poised to pounce and would like nothing better than to catch you napping. Keep your guard up. You're not the only ones plunged into these hard times. It's the same with Christians all over the world. So keep a firm grip on the faith. The suffering won't last forever. It won't be long

before this generous God who has great plans for us in Christ—eternal and glorious plans they are!—will have you put together and on your feet for good. He gets the last word; yes, he does.

Romans 8:18 (KJV)

18 For I reckon that the sufferings of this present time are not worthy to be compared with the glory which shall be revealed in us.

Everyone has had to go through some fires in their lives. What keeps us going is knowing that we may have to experience some suffering in our lives but we don't have stay there—we go through. The goal is to go through victoriously.

We can boldly say, I've been through hell . . . BUT GOD!

James 1:2-12 (MSG)

2-4 Consider it a sheer gift, friends, when tests and challenges come at you from all sides. You know that under pressure, your faith-life is forced into the open and shows its true colors. So don't try to get out of anything prematurely. Let it do its work so you become mature and well-developed, not deficient in any way.

5-8 If you don't know what you're doing, pray to the Father. He loves to help. You'll get his help, and won't be condescended to when you ask for it. Ask boldly, believingly, without a second thought. People who "worry their prayers" are like wind-whipped waves. Don't think you're going to get anything from the Master that way, adrift at sea, keeping all your options open.

9-11 When down-and-outers get a break, cheer! And when the arrogant rich are brought down to size, cheer! Prosperity is as short-lived as a wildflower, so don't ever count on it. You know that as soon as the sun rises, pouring down its scorching heat, the flower withers. Its petals wilt and, before you know it, that beautiful face is a barren stem. Well, that's a picture of the "prosperous life." At the very moment everyone is looking on in admiration, it fades away to nothing.

12 Anyone who meets a testing challenge head-on and manages to stick it out is mighty fortunate. For such persons loyally in love with God, the reward is life and more life.

25

Going to Hell in a hand basket

You are in extremely bad state and becoming worse. headed for complete disaster.

In the Spirit "Going to hell in a hand basket"

DEEP CLEANING MY HOUSE—

Because this world was on its' way to hell, God sent His son Jesus to die for our sins that we may have eternal life through Him.

John 3:16-18 (KJV)

[16] For God so loved the world, that he gave his only begotten Son, that whosoever believeth in him should not perish, but have everlasting life.

[17] For God sent not his Son into the world to condemn the world; but that the world through him might be saved.

[18] He that believeth on him is not condemned: but he that believeth not is condemned already, because he hath not believed in the name of the only begotten Son of God.

After King David had sinned…. His prayer was…

Psalm 51:4-6 (KJV)

[4] Against thee, thee only, have I sinned, and done this evil in thy sight: that thou mightest be justified when thou speakest, and be clear when thou judgest.

[5] Behold, I was shapen in iniquity; and in sin did my mother conceive me.

[6] Behold, thou desirest truth in the inward parts: and in the hidden part thou shalt make me to know wisdom.

26

Crazy as hell

This phrase can be used as a compliment or insult. On one hand it can mean, you have totally lost your mind—you are deranged and on the other hand it can mean "you are so funny or silly".

"Crazy" is used as a modifier like "extremely" or "intensely"; it means irrational or unexplainable; People sometimes use the word "crazy" to mean silly, strange, or outlandish. Although this phrase is sometimes used to describe mental illness, I do not associate the phrase with describing the disease.

In the Spirit "Crazy as hell"

DEEP CLEANING MY HOUSE—

James 1:5 - 8 (KJV)

⁵ If any of you lack wisdom, let him ask of God, that giveth to all men liberally, and upbraideth not; and it shall be given him.

⁶ But let him ask in faith, nothing wavering. For he that wavereth is like a wave of the sea driven with the wind and tossed.

⁷ For let not that man think that he shall receive any thing of the Lord.

⁸ A double minded man is unstable in all his ways.

27

To Hell with it

This phrase typically comes out when a person is sick and tired of being sick and tired— he or she is done fighting and doesn't want to expend any more energy into trying to fix the problem. It's over!

It means "I wash my hands of this person, this situation—It is what it is… I'm not thinking nothing else about it—I'm not going to beat a dead horse anymore— IT'S A WRAP! IT'S OVER.

In the Spirit "To hell with it"

DEEP CLEANING MY HOUSE—

To hell with it comes at a time when a person has reached his or her wits end. As a child of God, I'm reminded of the story of the prodigal son. After leaving his father's house, spending all his riches, and living in the pigpen, worse than an animal, he came to himself.

Just like when we finally realize who we are as children of God and say, *"I don't have to live like hell— I'm going back home to my Father's house."*

Luke 15:11-24 (MSG)

The Story of the Lost Son

¹¹⁻¹² Then he said, "There was once a man who had two sons. The younger said to his father, 'Father, I want right now what's coming to me.'

¹²⁻¹⁶ "So the father divided the property between them. It wasn't long before the younger son packed his bags and left for a distant country. There, undisciplined and dissipated, he wasted everything he had. After he had gone through all his money, there was a bad famine all through that country and he began to feel it. He signed on with a citizen there who assigned him to his fields to slop the pigs. He was so hungry he would have eaten the

corn-cobs in the pig slop, but no one would give him any.

17-20 "That brought him to his senses. He said, 'All those farmhands working for my father sit down to three meals a day, and here I am starving to death. I'm going back to my father. I'll say to him, Father, I've sinned against God, I've sinned before you; I don't deserve to be called your son. Take me on as a hired hand.' He got right up and went home to his father.

20-21 "When he was still a long way off, his father saw him. His heart pounding, he ran out, embraced him, and kissed him. The son started his speech: 'Father, I've sinned against God, I've sinned before you; I don't deserve to be called your son ever again.'

22-24 "But the father wasn't listening. He was calling to the servants, 'Quick. Bring a clean set of clothes and dress him. Put the family ring on his finger and sandals on his feet. Then get a prize-winning heifer and roast it. We're going to feast! We're going to have a wonderful time! My son is here—given up for dead and now alive! Given up for lost and now found!' And they began to have a wonderful time.

28

Come hell or high water

Determination— I will do this thing no matter what comes— Something will happen no matter how difficult it is— no matter if it's fire or flood, I WILL… IT WILL…

Blinders are placed on the eyes of racehorses to make them focus on what is ahead, rather than what is at the side or behind— keeping them focused when racing round a racecourse. A hell or high-water mentality is like a race horse pressing towards the prize. It doesn't matter what is going on around—the focus is on the goal.

In the Spirit "Come hell or high water"

DEEP CLEANING MY HOUSE—

Come hell or high water in the Spirit focuses on building our firm foundation upon Christ so that we can withstand the storms of life.

Matthew 7:24-26 (KJV)

²⁴ Therefore whosoever heareth these sayings of mine, and doeth them, I will liken him unto a wise man, which built his house upon a rock:

²⁵ And the rain descended, and the floods came, and the winds blew, and beat upon that house; and it fell not: for it was founded upon a rock.

²⁶ And every one that heareth these sayings of mine, and doeth them not, shall be likened unto a foolish man, which built his house upon the sand:

Luke 6:47-49 (KJV)

⁴⁷ Whosoever cometh to me, and heareth my sayings, and doeth them, I will shew you to whom he is like:

⁴⁸ He is like a man which built an house, and digged deep, and laid the foundation on a rock: and when the flood arose, the stream beat vehemently upon that house, and could not shake it: for it was founded upon a rock.

⁴⁹ But he that heareth, and doeth not, is like a man that without a foundation built an house upon the earth; against which the stream did beat vehemently, and immediately it fell; and the ruin of that house was great.

There is a song called *"My Soul has been Anchored,"* by the late Douglas Miller that was recorded in 1985 on his album, *"Unspeakable Joy"* album.

The song talks about the raging storms in the writer's life. He share that the storms are coming so strongly that it's hard for him to tell the night from day (meaning the bad times are overpowering the good times in his life so much so that the line has become blurred).

Although the writer expresses that the storm (or life's trials and tests appear unbearable), he shares a bit of hope in the midst of that terrible place that he is in. He talks about his soul being anchored in the Lord.

These words are not only the writer sharing his experience but the words are also a direct reflection of scripture.

Hebrews 6:17-20 (KJV)

17 Wherein God, willing more abundantly to shew unto the heirs of promise the immutability of his counsel, confirmed it by an oath:

18 That by two immutable things, in which it was impossible for God to lie, we might have a strong consolation, who have fled for refuge to lay hold upon the hope set before us:

19 Which hope we have as an anchor of the soul, both sure and stedfast, and which entereth into that within the veil;

20 Whither the forerunner is for us entered, even Jesus, made an high priest for ever after the order of Melchisedec.

Towards the end of "My Soul has been anchored", the lyrics share about having that anchor "in the Word of God", which keeps him "steadfast and unmovable". The song is a beautiful reminder and exhortation for believers to rely upon the stable force in our lives.

The Word of God—both the written word and living Word (a direct manifestation of the mind and will of God). It is encouraging to know that even in the midst of the storm— God's got us!
In the midst of hell and high water, I've got an anchor. My anchor is built upon that firm foundation, as described in Luke 6:47-49.

1 Corinthians 15:57-58 (KJV)

⁵⁷ But thanks be to God, which giveth us the victory through our Lord Jesus Christ.

⁵⁸ Therefore, my beloved brethren, be ye stedfast, unmoveable, always abounding in the work of the Lord, forasmuch as ye know that your labour is not in vain in the Lord.

I have a song that I wrote called "In the Midst of the Storm (You are my keeper)" that was recorded in

2002 on my "Soul of a Sister" CD. It's my reminder that no matter what storms I face, I must always remember that I am kept safe in the arms of Jesus and there's some things that I must do when the hell and high water come.

Call: You are my keeper,
    my guide
    my strong tower

Response: In the midst of the storm.
(Repeat call/response 4x)

Call: I praise   **Response:** (I praise)
Call: Your name   **Response:** (your name)
(Repeat call/response 4x)

Lord we praise you in the midst of the storm
Lord we praise you, you'll keep us safe from harm.

Call: You are my keeper   Response: You are my keeper
Call: You are my guide   Response: You are my guide

In the midst of the storm
In the midst of the storm

In the midst of the storm you are my keeper.

29

Hellish

Extremely unpleasant; vile

In the Spirit "Hellish"

DEEP CLEANING MY HOUSE—

Vile means anything that is morally bad or wicked. The numerous synonyms that describe this word are:

God does not want us to be hellish—or vile! This word speaks to the character or core of an individual. Our character and our way of life should be like Jesus.

The Word of God tells us to "be holy".

1 Peter 1:13-17 (MSG)

A Future in God

¹³⁻¹⁶ So roll up your sleeves, get your head in the game, be totally ready to receive the gift that's coming when Jesus arrives. Don't lazily slip back into those old grooves of evil, doing just what you feel like doing. You didn't know any better then; you do now. As obedient children, let yourselves be pulled into a way of life shaped by God's life, a life energetic and blazing with holiness. God said, "I am holy; you be holy."

¹⁷ You call out to God for help and he helps—he's a good Father that way. But don't forget, he's also a responsible Father, and won't let you get by with sloppy living.

The scripture that really stands out for me in the Word of God is when God first called the boy Samuel and spoke to him. This was the first time that God had spoke to the young boy, so God had to call Samuel several times before, Eli (Samuel's guardian) perceived that it was God calling the boy.

When God spoke to Samuel, it was to reveal to the boy what His plans were because Eli had allowed his sons' *vile* behavior go unchecked in the house of God.

1 Samuel 3 (MSG)

"Speak, God. I'm Ready to Listen"

3 ¹⁻³ The boy Samuel was serving God under Eli's direction. This was at a time when the revelation of God was rarely heard or seen. One night Eli was sound asleep (his eyesight was very bad—he could hardly see). It was well before dawn; the sanctuary lamp was still burning. Samuel was still in bed in the Temple of God, where the Chest of God rested.

⁴⁻⁵ Then God called out, "Samuel, Samuel!"

Samuel answered, "Yes? I'm here." Then he ran to Eli saying, "I heard you call. Here I am."

Eli said, "I didn't call you. Go back to bed." And so he did.

6-7 GOD called again, "Samuel, Samuel!"

Samuel got up and went to Eli, "I heard you call. Here I am."

Again Eli said, "Son, I didn't call you. Go back to bed." (This all happened before Samuel knew GOD for himself. It was before the revelation of GOD had been given to him personally.)

8-9 GOD called again, "Samuel!"—the third time! Yet again Samuel got up and went to Eli, "Yes? I heard you call me. Here I am."

That's when it dawned on Eli that GOD was calling the boy. So Eli directed Samuel, "Go back and lie down. If the voice calls again, say, 'Speak, GOD. I'm your servant, ready to listen.'" Samuel returned to his bed.

10 Then GOD came and stood before him exactly as before, calling out, "Samuel! Samuel!"

Samuel answered, "Speak. I'm your servant, ready to listen."

11-14 GOD said to Samuel, "Listen carefully. I'm getting ready to do something in Israel that is going to shake everyone up and get their attention. The time has come for me to bring down on Eli's family everything I warned him of, every last word of it. I'm letting him know that the time's up. I'm bringing judgment on his family for good. He knew what was going on, that his sons were desecrating God's name and God's place, and he did nothing to stop them. This is my sentence on the family of Eli: The evil of Eli's family can never be wiped out by sacrifice or offering."

15 Samuel stayed in bed until morning, then rose early and went about his duties, opening the doors of the sanctuary, but he dreaded having to tell the vision to Eli.

16 But then Eli summoned Samuel: "Samuel, my son!"

Samuel came running: "Yes? What can I do for you?"

17 "What did he say? Tell it to me, all of it. Don't suppress or soften one word, as God is your judge! I want it all, word for word as he said it to you."

18 So Samuel told him, word for word. He held back nothing.

Eli said, "He is GOD. Let him do whatever he thinks best."

19-21 Samuel grew up. GOD was with him, and Samuel's prophetic record was flawless. Everyone in Israel, from Dan in the north to Beersheba in the south, recognized that Samuel was the real thing—a true prophet of GOD. GOD continued to show up at Shiloh, revealed through his word to Samuel at Shiloh.

As we are nearing the close of identifying *"Hell Chapters"* in our lives that need to be conquered, it is important for us to learn how to hear the voice of God. Our Heavenly father speaks to us through His Word, through dreams and visions— and there are many of us who audibly hear His voice calling.

Will we answer?

30

Tired as Hell

Tired as hell means that you are weary, worn out—exhausted from work or a mental or physical burden.

In the Spirit "Tired as Hell"

DEEP CLEANING MY HOUSE—

It is important to know that we are not alone in this battle or in this race. The bible encourages us to lay aside the weight and sin and focus on Jesus.

Hebrews 12:1-3 (KJV)

12 Wherefore seeing we also are compassed about with so great a cloud of witnesses, let us lay aside every weight, and the sin which doth so easily beset us, and let us run with patience the race that is set before us,

² Looking unto Jesus the author and finisher of our faith; who for the joy that was set before him endured the cross, despising the shame, and is set down at the right hand of the throne of God.

³ For consider him that endured such contradiction of sinners against himself, lest ye be wearied and faint in your minds.

Hebrews 12:1-3 (MSG)
Discipline in a Long-Distance Race

12 ¹⁻³ Do you see what this means—all these pioneers who blazed the way, all these veterans cheering us on? It means we'd better get on with it. Strip down, start running—and never quit! No extra spiritual fat, no parasitic sins. Keep your eyes on *Jesus*, who both began and finished this race we're in. Study how he did it. Because he never lost sight of where he was headed—that exhilarating finish in and with God—he could put up with anything along the way: Cross, shame, whatever.

And now he's *there*, in the place of honor, right alongside God. When you find yourselves flagging in your faith, go over that story again, item by item, that long litany of hostility he plowed through. *That* will shoot adrenaline into your souls!

Knowing that God has not brought us this far in the battle or race to leave us is comforting and it is essential that we comfort and encourage ourselves with the Word of God. READ IT. MEDITATE ON IT. STUDY IT—and most of all KNOW IT.

Isaiah 40:29-31 (KJV)

²⁹ He giveth power to the faint; and to them that have no might he increaseth strength.

³⁰ Even the youths shall faint and be weary, and the young men shall utterly fall:

³¹ But they that wait upon the Lord shall renew their strength; they shall mount up with wings as eagles; they shall run, and not be weary; and they shall walk, and not faint.

# ANNIE RUTH

Part 2
Going
Deeper

Courage

Courage is not just defined by large acts, courage is also demonstrated in small acts of *"facing and pressing through trials, despite our fears or hardships."*

Courage is the quality shown by someone who decides to do something difficult or dangerous even though that person may be afraid.

During the season of writing this book, I was empowered by God and I embraced the courage to stand strong in the midst of the fire. It doesn't mean that times didn't get hard, but I persevered.

Courage is not the absence of fear but the triumph over it— pressing on in spite of the battle that exists. The brave person is not the one who does not feel afraid, but the brave person is the one who conquers that fear.

I'm reminded of the scripture that we are more than conquerors. To conquer means to overcome and take control of *(a place, a people, or a circumstance)* by military force. To conquer is to successfully overcome a problem or weakness.

Conquering is climbing a mountain successfully. This can be a physical mountain or a metaphorical mountain in our lives.

Conquering is manifested in our minds and our thought process.

Romans 8:28-31 (KJV)

28 And we know that all things work together for good to them that love God, to them who are the called according to his purpose.

29 For whom he did foreknow, he also did predestinate to be conformed to the image of his Son, that he might be the firstborn among many brethren.

30 Moreover whom he did predestinate, them he also called: and whom he called, them he also justified: and whom he justified, them he also glorified.

31 What shall we then say to these things? If God be for us, who can be against us?

Knowing that we are conquerors allows us to

embrace courage and make a conscious choice to be courageous.

Courage is a choice to face or confront agony, pain, danger, uncertainty, and intimidation. It is a state of mind and a willingness to fight regardless of the consequences or limitations.

Courage is seeing beyond the obstacles and looking to Jesus— the author and finisher of our faith.

Fear

Fear is an unpleasant, often strong emotion caused by anticipation or awareness of danger. Fear is also a profound reverence and awe especially toward God.

Some synonyms for FEAR are fright, alarm, panic, terror, and insecurity. Fear implies anxiety and loss of courage. In the context of this book, I will mainly use the definition of FEAR as timid, worry, anxiety.

When you're facing the unknown and have no idea of what the outcome will be, but you trust God that he is faithful, and you are safe in His arms. There are scriptures that I meditate on.

Psalm 91 (KJV)

He that dwelleth in the secret place of the most High shall abide under the shadow of the Almighty.

[2] I will say of the Lord, He is my refuge and my fortress: my God; in him will I trust.

³ Surely he shall deliver thee from the snare of the fowler, and from the noisome pestilence.

⁴ He shall cover thee with his feathers, and under his wings shalt thou trust: his truth shall be thy shield and buckler.

⁵ Thou shalt not be afraid for the terror by night; nor for the arrow that flieth by day;

⁶ Nor for the pestilence that walketh in darkness; nor for the destruction that wasteth at noonday.

⁷ A thousand shall fall at thy side, and ten thousand at thy right hand; but it shall not come nigh thee.

⁸ Only with thine eyes shalt thou behold and see the reward of the wicked.

⁹ Because thou hast made the LORD, which is my refuge, even the most High, thy habitation;

¹⁰ There shall no evil befall thee, neither shall any plague come nigh thy dwelling.

¹¹ For he shall give his angels charge over thee, to keep thee in all thy ways.

¹² They shall bear thee up in their hands, lest thou dash thy foot against a stone.

¹³ Thou shalt tread upon the lion and adder: the young lion and the dragon shalt thou trample under feet.

¹⁴ Because he hath set his love upon me, therefore will I deliver him: I will set him on high, because he hath known my name.

¹⁵ He shall call upon me, and I will answer him: I will be with him in trouble; I will deliver him, and honour him.

¹⁶ With long life will I satisfy him, and shew him my salvation.

Under Fire (Under Attack)

Being under attack or under fire means that you are subjected to the attack of the enemy. Courage under fire is bravery while still being shot at. You are still moving forward to change things although opposition exists.

During this time, we are subject to aggressive, violent, or hurtful action; we are being acted against and are in literally in WAR. There are several types of attacks that can and will occur at some point in our lives. The enemy uses various schemes and battle tactics against us. But we must always realize that we win the war— and the battle is not ours, it's the Lord's. God will give us how to fight the enemy and we will and can overcome.

Recognizing the type of attack When you're <u>UNDER FIRE</u>

The enemy uses specific types of attacks for every individual. The areas that I am attacked in are different from the areas that my sister or brother may be attacked in. The types of attacks are as follows:

- **Bombarded** = continuously with bombs, shells, and missiles.
- **Assault** = physical attack, verbal attack, or sudden intense violence.
- **Assail** = repeated attacks.
- **Storm** = disturbed state of environment (severe weather). In **Mark 4:37-40** Jesus said, *"Peace be still"* to the storm. We have that same power to speak to storms in our lives.
- **Beset** = attacked from all sides (covered with trouble or threatened persistently).

Mark 4:37-40 (KJV)

37 And there arose a great storm of wind, and the waves beat into the ship, so that it was now full.

38 And he was in the hinder part of the ship, asleep on a

pillow: and they awake him, and say unto him, Master, carest thou not that we perish?

⁳⁹ And he arose, and rebuked the wind, and said unto the sea, Peace, be still. And the wind ceased, and there was a great calm.

⁴⁰ And he said unto them, Why are ye so fearful? how is it that ye have no faith?

There is a song that I used to listen to that was written and recorded by the late Bishop Walter Hawkins on his "Love Alive II album called "There's a war going on." The song is a reminder to the believer that we are in a war and we have to be equipped with the Word of God.

The song reminds us that Word of God has to be deep within us. The Word of God isn't only our weapon but it is our food— our source – our strength. The song reenforces to us that the war that we are fighting can't be won with "bullets and guns". In summation the song reminds us that we have to be rooted and grounded in the Word of God.

2 Corinthians 10:3-5 (KJV)

³ For though we walk in the flesh, we do not war after the flesh:

⁴ (For the weapons of our warfare are not carnal, but mighty through God to the pulling down of strong holds;)

⁵ Casting down imaginations, and every high thing that exalteth itself against the knowledge of God, and bringing into captivity every thought to the obedience of Christ;

2 Corinthians 10:3-6 (MSG)

³⁻⁶ The world is unprincipled. It's dog-eat-dog out there! The world doesn't fight fair. But we don't live or fight our battles that way—never have and never will. The tools of our trade aren't for marketing or manipulation, but they are for demolishing that entire massively corrupt culture. We use our powerful God-tools for smashing warped philosophies, tearing down barriers erected against the truth of God, fitting every loose thought and emotion and impulse into the structure of life shaped by Christ. Our tools are ready at hand for

clearing the ground of every obstruction and building lives of obedience into maturity.

The Fire

FIRE = combustion, burning.
[Verb] discharge a gun or other weapon in order to explosively propel (fiery darts of the enemy).

[Noun] shooting projectiles from weapons, especially bullets from guns.

Fire is hot but we must keep in mind that there are two different types of fire. The fire meant to destroy us and the fire meant to cleanse us. The cleansing fire is often referred to as the refiner's fire. This is the fire that God allows us to go through to purify our hearts.

Refiner. noun. a person, device, or substance that removes impurities, sediment, or other unwanted matter from something.

Job 23:9-11 (KJV)

⁹ On the left hand, where he doth work, but I cannot behold him: he hideth himself on the right hand, that I cannot see him:

¹⁰ But he knoweth the way that I take: when he hath tried me, I shall come forth as gold.

¹¹ My foot hath held his steps, his way have I kept, and not declined.

Example: How gold is purified in the fire (impurities rise to the top of the molten metal). The process of this refining fire can also be demonstrated through the testing of our faith. God knows what is in us, however we are tested to see ourselves and where we need to grow and develop.

James 1:2-8 (KJV)

² My brethren, count it all joy when ye fall into divers temptations;

³ Knowing this, that the trying of your faith worketh patience.

⁴ But let patience have her perfect work, that ye may be perfect and entire, wanting nothing.

⁵ If any of you lack wisdom, let him ask of God, that giveth to all men liberally, and upbraideth not; and it shall be given him.

⁶ But let him ask in faith, nothing wavering. For he that wavereth is like a wave of the sea driven with the wind and tossed.

⁷ For let not that man think that he shall receive any thing of the Lord.

⁸ A double minded man is unstable in all his ways.

During this testing we must be sure to fast and pray. There are times in our lives that we've got to acknowledge that "… this kind cometh not out but by prayer and fasting".

Matthew 17:14-21 (KJV)

¹⁴ And when they were come to the multitude, there came to him a certain man, kneeling down to him, and saying,

¹⁵ Lord, have mercy on my son: for he is lunatick, and sore vexed: for ofttimes he falleth into the fire, and oft into the water.

¹⁶ And I brought him to thy disciples, and they could not cure him.

¹⁷ Then Jesus answered and said, O faithless and perverse generation, how long shall I be with you? how long shall I suffer you? bring him hither to me.

¹⁸ And Jesus rebuked the devil; and he departed out of him: and the child was cured from that very hour.

¹⁹ Then came the disciples to Jesus apart, and said, Why could not we cast him out?

²⁰ And Jesus said unto them, Because of your unbelief: for verily I say unto you, If ye have faith as a grain of mustard seed, ye shall say unto this mountain, Remove hence to yonder place; and it shall remove; and nothing shall be impossible unto you.

²¹ Howbeit this kind goeth not out but by prayer and fasting.

STOP, DROP, AND ROLL

In the natural sense if our clothing catches on fire, we are taught to "stop, drop and roll".

In the spiritual sense that lesson applies as well. When you are going through the fires of life, you have to **STOP, DROP AND ROLL.**

STOP (PRAISE) **DROP** (PRAY) **ROLL** (PROCEED)

- **STOP** and do not do anything in your emotions.
- **DROP** on your knees and pray
- **ROLL** through the storm—keep moving onward and upward in Christ Jesus because God will carry you through it.

When going through the fire, I have learned to encourage myself with the Word of God.

Psalm 46 (KJV)

God is our refuge and strength, a very present help in trouble.

² Therefore will not we fear, though the earth be removed, and though the mountains be carried into the midst of the sea;

³ Though the waters thereof roar and be troubled, though the mountains shake with the swelling thereof. Selah.

⁴ There is a river, the streams whereof shall make glad the city of God, the holy place of the tabernacles of the most High.

⁵ God is in the midst of her; she shall not be moved: God shall help her, and that right early.

⁶ The heathen raged, the kingdoms were moved: he uttered his voice, the earth melted.

⁷ The Lord of hosts is with us; the God of Jacob is our refuge. Selah.

⁸ Come, behold the works of the Lord, what desolations he hath made in the earth.

⁹ He maketh wars to cease unto the end of the earth; he breaketh the bow, and cutteth the spear in sunder; he burneth the chariot in the fire.

¹⁰ Be still, and know that I am God: I will be exalted among the heathen, I will be exalted in the earth.

¹¹ The Lord of hosts is with us; the God of Jacob is our refuge. Selah.

Activating the Principles of STOP, DROP AND ROLL

STOP It is important not to do anything or make any major decisions in your emotions. During this time of stopping, we must be still and wait. That means, depending on the situation, there is a time to **stop** *(do not move forward— do not knock that person across the head— do not cuss that person out, etc.)*

However, stopping doesn't mean that you are not doing anything. Waiting and being still means that we are praising God in the midst of whatever we are going through—we are praising God despite what we are going through and we are standing still and seeing the salvation of the Lord.

We are given a good description of what *waiting* looks like. Oftentimes waiting looks different but it has the same outcome— THAT GOD WILL GET THE GLORY!

Psalm 46:10 (KJV)

¹⁰ Be still, and know that I am God: I will be exalted among the heathen, I will be exalted in the earth.

Waiting is sometimes passive and sometimes active. An active wait means that I am praising God in the midst of the circumstance. I am earnestly hoping with great expectation.

Isaiah 40:31 (KJV)

³¹ But they that wait upon the LORD shall renew their strength; they shall mount up with wings as eagles; they shall run, and not be weary; and they shall walk, and not faint.

Stop also means to stand still, move yourself out of the way and let God control and guide the situation. In Exodus, when Pharoah's army was pursuing the children of Israel, Moses exhorted the people.

Exodus 14:13-14 (KJV)

¹³ And Moses said unto the people, Fear ye not, stand still, and see the salvation of the Lord, which he will shew to you to day: for the Egyptians whom ye have seen to day, ye shall see them again no more for ever.

¹⁴ The Lord shall fight for you, and ye shall hold your peace.

BACKGROUND ON STANDING STILL

2 Chronicles 20 really touches my heart. It demonstrates how God instructed his people to stand still but in the midst of their standing still—they were praising God. That posture of standing still and praising still holds true today. When we face the trials of life, as God's daughter

or son, our instructions are *"stand still and see the salvation of the Lord"*.

2 Chronicles 20:1-28 (MSG)

20 ¹⁻² Some time later the Moabites and Ammonites, accompanied by Meunites, joined forces to make war on Jehoshaphat. Jehoshaphat received this intelligence report: "A huge force is on its way from beyond the Dead Sea to fight you. There's no time to waste—they're already at Hazazon Tamar, the oasis of En Gedi."

³⁻⁴ Shaken, Jehoshaphat prayed. He went to GOD for help and ordered a nationwide fast. The country of Judah united in seeking GOD's help—they came from all the cities of Judah to pray to GOD.

⁵⁻⁹ Then Jehoshaphat took a position before the assembled people of Judah and Jerusalem at The Temple of GOD in front of the new courtyard and said, "O GOD, God of our ancestors, are you not God in heaven above and ruler of all kingdoms below? You hold all power and might in your fist—no one stands a chance against you! And didn't you make the natives of this land leave as you brought your people Israel in, turning it over permanently to your people Israel, the descendants of

CONQUERING THE HELL CHAPTERS

Abraham your friend? They have lived here and built a holy house of worship to honor you, saying, 'When the worst happens—whether war or flood or disease or famine—and we take our place before this Temple (we know you are personally present in this place!) and pray out our pain and trouble, we know that you will listen and give victory.'

10-12 "And now it's happened: men from Ammon, Moab, and Mount Seir have shown up. You didn't let Israel touch them when we got here at first—we detoured around them and didn't lay a hand on them. And now they've come to kick us out of the country you gave us. O dear God, won't you take care of them? We're helpless before this vandal horde ready to attack us. We don't know what to do; we're looking to you."

13 Everyone in Judah was there—little children, wives, sons—all present and attentive to GOD.

14-17 Then Jahaziel was moved by the Spirit of GOD to speak from the midst of the congregation. (Jahaziel was the son of Zechariah, the son of Benaiah, the son of Jeiel, the son of Mattaniah the Levite of the Asaph clan.) He said, "Attention everyone—all of you from out of town, all you from Jerusalem, and you King Jehoshaphat—GOD's word: Don't be afraid; don't pay any mind to this vandal horde. This is God's war, not yours. Tomorrow you'll go after them; see, they're already on their way up the slopes of Ziz; you'll meet them at the end of the ravine near the wilderness of Jeruel. You won't have to lift a hand in this battle; just stand firm, Judah and Jerusalem, and watch GOD's saving work for you take shape. Don't be afraid, don't waver. March out boldly tomorrow—GOD is with you."

¹⁸⁻¹⁹ Then Jehoshaphat knelt down, bowing with his face to the ground. All Judah and Jerusalem did the same, worshiping GOD. The Levites (both Kohathites and Korahites) stood to their feet to praise GOD, the God of Israel; they praised at the top of their lungs!

²⁰ They were up early in the morning, ready to march into the wilderness of Tekoa. As they were leaving, Jehoshaphat stood up and said, "Listen Judah and Jerusalem! Listen to what I have to say! Believe firmly in GOD, your God, and your lives will be firm! Believe in your prophets and you'll come out on top!"

²¹ After talking it over with the people, Jehoshaphat appointed a choir for GOD; dressed in holy robes, they were to march ahead of the troops, singing,

> **Give thanks to GOD,**
> **His love never quits.**

22-23 As soon as they started shouting and praising, GOD set ambushes against the men of Ammon, Moab, and Mount Seir as they were attacking Judah, and they all ended up dead. The Ammonites and Moabites mistakenly attacked those from Mount Seir and massacred them. Then, further confused, they went at each other, and all ended up killed.

24 As Judah came up over the rise, looking into the wilderness for the horde of barbarians, they looked on a killing field of dead bodies—not a living soul among them.

25-26 When Jehoshaphat and his people came to carry off the plunder they found more loot than they could carry off—equipment, clothing, valuables. It took three days to cart it away! On the fourth day they came together at the Valley of Blessing (Beracah) and blessed GOD (that's how it got the name, Valley of Blessing).

27-28 Jehoshaphat then led all the men of Judah and Jerusalem back to Jerusalem—an exuberant parade. GOD had given them joyful relief from their enemies! They entered Jerusalem and came to The Temple of GOD with all the instruments of the band playing

DROP means to go into prayer. Prayer is talking with God— a reverent communication that requires speaking and mostly listening. There are many postures of prayer, but they all have one thing in common— a humbleness of heart and spirit towards our Heavenly Father.

The Word of God encourages us to pray.

Psalm 91 (KJV)

91 He that dwelleth in the secret place of the most High shall abide under the shadow of the Almighty.

2 I will say of the LORD, He is my refuge and my fortress: my God; in him will I trust.

3 Surely he shall deliver thee from the snare of the fowler, and from the noisome pestilence.

4 He shall cover thee with his feathers, and under his wings shalt thou trust: his truth shall be thy shield and buckler.

5 Thou shalt not be afraid for the terror by night; nor for the arrow that flieth by day;

6 Nor for the pestilence that walketh in darkness; nor for the destruction that wasteth at noonday.

7 A thousand shall fall at thy side, and ten thousand at thy right hand; but it shall not come nigh thee.

⁸ Only with thine eyes shalt thou behold and see the reward of the wicked.

⁹ Because thou hast made the LORD, which is my refuge, even the most High, thy habitation;

¹⁰ There shall no evil befall thee, neither shall any plague come nigh thy dwelling.

¹¹ For he shall give his angels charge over thee, to keep thee in all thy ways.

¹² They shall bear thee up in their hands, lest thou dash thy foot against a stone.

¹³ Thou shalt tread upon the lion and adder: the young lion and the dragon shalt thou trample under feet.

¹⁴ Because he hath set his love upon me, therefore will I deliver him: I will set him on high, because he hath known my name.

¹⁵ He shall call upon me, and I will answer him: I will be with him in trouble; I will deliver him, and honour him.

16 With long life will I satisfy him, and shew him my salvation.

When we learn to look at prayer as that reverent conversation with God—Our Father, then it doesn't seem strange to us. The Word of God encourages us to seek Him early. If we look at prayer as receiving our battle instructions or morning briefing then we know that prayer is, as essential as breathing and effectively implementing the plan that God has established for us.
The Word of God says,

Psalm 63:1-3 (KJV)

O God, thou art my God; early will I seek thee: my soul thirsteth for thee, my flesh longeth for thee in a dry and thirsty land, where no water is;

2 To see thy power and thy glory, so as I have seen thee in the sanctuary.

3 Because thy lovingkindness is better than life, my lips shall praise thee.

When I was little girl, my first exposure to talking to God was kneeling by my bedside to say my nighttime prayers or blessing my food at the kitchen table before we ate our meal. In my mind, prayer had two major postures. *"Sitting and kneeling"*. As I grew older and grew in the Lord, I learned that there are many postures of prayer. It is our *soul and spirit* that we bow in humble submission to our Heavenly Father. Oftentimes this posture will manifest itself in different physical positions.

POSTURES OF PRAYER

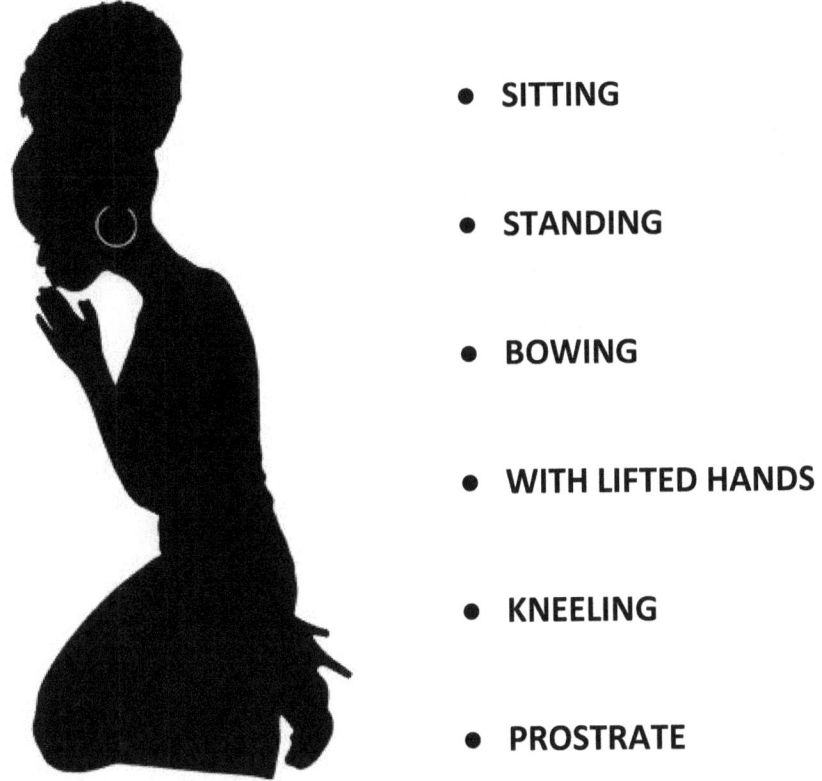

- SITTING

- STANDING

- BOWING

- WITH LIFTED HANDS

- KNEELING

- PROSTRATE

The last principle to activate when one is conquering the hell chapters is TO ROLL.

ROLL means to *(keep moving forward)* to *go through the fire—* through the test, as God would have you to go through it. It doesn't mean that you don't feel emotions like anger, pain, uncertainty, regret and so many other feelings but going through (ROLLING) means that you're going not going to stay in that place that will defeat you. If you are in the fire, it is not a place of permanency; you will not be burned.

So, when my friend stated, "You don't smell like what you've been through", I clearly understood what she was saying to me. Herein is the testimony of Shadrach (Hannaniah), Meshach (Mishael), and Abednego (Azariah).

Daniel 3:15 - 28 (KJV)

[15] Now if ye be ready that at what time ye hear the sound of the cornet, flute, harp, sackbut, psaltery, and dulcimer, and all kinds of musick, ye fall down and worship the image which I have made; well: but if ye worship not, ye shall be cast the same hour into the midst of a burning fiery furnace; and who is that God that shall deliver you out of my hands?

[16] Shadrach, Meshach, and Abednego, answered and said to the king, O Nebuchadnezzar, we are not careful to answer thee in this matter.

17 If it be so, our God whom we serve is able to deliver us from the burning fiery furnace, and he will deliver us out of thine hand, O king.

18 But if not, be it known unto thee, O king, that we will not serve thy gods, nor worship the golden image which thou hast set up.

19 Then was Nebuchadnezzar full of fury, and the form of his visage was changed against Shadrach, Meshach, and Abednego: therefore he spake, and commanded that they should heat the furnace one seven times more than it was wont to be heated.

20 And he commanded the most mighty men that were in his army to bind Shadrach, Meshach, and Abednego, and to cast them into the burning fiery furnace.

21 Then these men were bound in their coats, their hosen, and their hats, and their other garments, and were cast into the midst of the burning fiery furnace.

22 Therefore because the king's commandment was urgent, and the furnace exceeding hot, the flames of the fire slew those men that took up Shadrach, Meshach, and Abednego.

²³ And these three men, Shadrach, Meshach, and Abednego, fell down bound into the midst of the burning fiery furnace.

²⁴ Then Nebuchadnezzar the king was astonished, and rose up in haste, and spake, and said unto his counsellors, Did not we cast three men bound into the midst of the fire? They answered and said unto the king, True, O king.

²⁵ He answered and said, Lo, I see four men loose, walking in the midst of the fire, and they have no hurt; and the form of the fourth is like the Son of God.

²⁶ Then Nebuchadnezzar came near to the mouth of the burning fiery furnace, and spake, and said, Shadrach, Meshach, and Abednego, ye servants of the most high God, come forth, and come hither. Then Shadrach, Meshach, and Abednego, came forth of the midst of the fire.

²⁷ And the princes, governors, and captains, and the king's counsellors, being gathered together, saw these men, upon whose bodies the fire had no power, nor was an hair of their head singed, neither were their coats changed, nor the smell of fire had passed on them.

28 Then Nebuchadnezzar spake, and said, Blessed be the God of Shadrach, Meshach, and Abednego, who hath sent his angel, and delivered his servants that trusted in him, and have changed the king's word, and yielded their bodies, that they might not serve nor worship any god, except their own God.

I am strengthened as I read and study the Word of God—I actively apply it to my everyday life. As a child, I also learned a very familiar scripture that assures me that I am not alone, and that God is with me—just like He was with Shadrach, Meshach, and Abednego.

Psalm 23 (KJV)

23 The LORD is my shepherd; I shall not want.

² He maketh me to lie down in green pastures: he leadeth me beside the still waters.

³ He restoreth my soul: he leadeth me in the paths of righteousness for his name's sake.

ANNIE RUTH

⁴ Yea, though I walk through the valley of the shadow of death, I will fear no evil: for thou art with me; thy rod and thy staff they comfort me.

⁵ Thou preparest a table before me in the presence of mine enemies: thou anointest my head with oil; my cup runneth over.

⁶ Surely goodness and mercy shall follow me all the days of my life: and I will dwell in the house of the LORD forever.

Although we often feel the physical effects of the battle, the major part of the battle occurs in our mind.

Rolling means that I must keep my mind focused on God. Rolling means that I am walking by faith and in that walk, I am walking with God. He is my focus, I seek His presence—he gives me the knowledge and wisdom—I am meditating on His Word. I am not worrying but I am walking in His peace—a peace that only He can give.

Philippians 4: 6– 9 (KJV)

⁶ Be careful for nothing; but in every thing by prayer and supplication with thanksgiving let your requests be made known unto God.

⁷ And the peace of God, which passeth all understanding, shall keep your hearts and minds through Christ Jesus.

⁸ Finally, brethren, whatsoever things are true, whatsoever things are honest, whatsoever things are just, whatsoever things are pure, whatsoever things are lovely, whatsoever things are of good report; if there be any virtue, and if there be any praise, think on these things.

⁹ Those things, which ye have both learned, and received, and heard, and seen in me, do: and the God of peace shall be with you.

Closing Words & Prayer

I am in awe of how God uses us as vessels. Never would I have imagined that the death of my mother would birth such a revelatory (prophetic, predictive, visionary) Word that speaks to my soul like none other. My prayer is that this Word has spoken to your soul as well.

Dear Father God,

I thank you for being the God who knows all— sees all— and is all powerful. You are not limited to what you do for your children. I pray that you heal every wounded heart. And like the Potter that you are— I pray that you make your children over— vessels fit for your use.

Let them know that the fire is not meant to destroy them and although they are tried within it, they will come out as pure gold. I pray a special blessing be upon everyone that reads these words that you have poured out of me. Please let your people know that I am simply the vessel that releases what you have poured into me. Sanctify each word. Let every word fall on good ground and let it minister to the deepest part of your children. In Jesus' name.

                                                                            Amen

www.ingramcontent.com/pod-product-compliance
Lightning Source LLC
Chambersburg PA
CBHW070547170426
43201CB00012B/1744